The Late Start

A No-Shame, No-Jargon Guide to Building Wealth After 40 — Even If You're Starting From Zero

Dr. Nathan Brookmire

The information in this book is provided for general informational and educational purposes only. It does not constitute professional, medical, or psychological advice. Readers are encouraged to consult qualified professionals for specific guidance.

Contents

Introduction: You're Not Behind. You're Starting.

Here is the thing about financial regret: it is exceptionally good at doing nothing useful while making you feel terrible.

You already know the math. You know about compound interest and time in the market and the fact that a twenty-five-year-old who saves $500 a month will end up with twice as much as a forty-five-year-old who saves the same amount. You've seen the charts. You've felt the weight of them. And none of that knowledge has produced a retirement account that matches where you feel like you should be.

So let's start with an honest acknowledgment: you missed some time. Maybe a lot of it. Maybe you spent your thirties paying off debt, or raising kids without a financial safety net, or working a job that covered the bills but left nothing for savings, or going through a divorce that reset everything, or simply living in a way that felt normal at the time and looks, in retrospect, like a missed opportunity. Maybe you knew better and didn't do it anyway. Maybe you didn't know better and wish someone had told you.

Any of that is behind you now. We're not going back to fix it.

What's in front of you is the relevant question. And the answer to that question is considerably better than the financial anxiety industry would have you believe.

Chapter 1: The Truth About Late Starters — What the Compound Interest Charts Don't Show You

Open any personal finance book written in the last thirty years and you'll find it on page one: the compound interest chart. It shows two investors — Early Ethel, who starts putting away $200 a month at age 22, and Late Larry, who waits until 40. By retirement, Early Ethel has $600,000. Late Larry has $140,000. The lesson is supposed to be motivating. Instead, it makes millions of people quietly close the book and walk away.

Here's what that chart is actually saying, underneath the financial math: You've already lost. Give up.

That's not motivation. That's shame dressed up as arithmetic.

The truth is more complicated — and more useful. Yes, time in the market matters enormously. Yes, starting at 22 gives you an advantage. But that chart leaves out everything that makes real human financial lives interesting: irregular income, the years you spent paying off student loans, the medical emergency that wiped out your savings, the decade you spent raising kids on one income, the divorce, the layoff, the years you were just trying to survive. It leaves out the fact that most people don't have $200 a month to spare at 22 — they have debt, entry-level wages, and no one in their family who ever talked about investing.

The compound interest chart is a perfectly accurate mathematical model applied to a life nobody actually lives.

So let's set it aside and talk about what's actually true for people who are starting at 40, 50, or even 60.

What the Research Actually Shows

Late starters are not a rare anomaly. According to Federal Reserve data, the median retirement savings for Americans between 44 and 49 is around $81,000. For those between 50 and 55, it's approximately $124,000. These numbers sound low — and by traditional benchmarks, they are — but they also represent tens of millions of people. If the "start at 22 or fail" narrative were the whole story, all those people would be financially doomed. They're not.

Studies on financial behavior consistently show that late starters often share a cluster of traits that give them real advantages over earlier savers:

Higher income potential. People in their 40s and 50s are typically at or near their peak earning years. The 28-year-old who couldn't find an extra $200 a month is now earning significantly more. That higher income means the capacity to save aggressively when it finally becomes possible.

Fewer financial distractions. Kids are older, or out of the house. The mortgage may be partially paid down. Some of the financial chaos of earlier life — the car payments, the daycare bills, the "I can't say no to this wedding in Cancun" expenses — has settled.

Clarity about priorities. People who start investing at 45 often do so with a sense of urgency that 25-year-olds simply don't feel. That urgency translates into focus. They don't dabble. They commit.

Better decision-making. Behavioral finance research shows that older investors tend to make fewer emotional trading decisions. The panic-selling and trend-chasing that destroys returns for younger investors is less common among people who have lived through enough market cycles to feel less rattled by them.

None of this cancels out the mathematical advantage of starting early. But it does mean that the picture is dramatically more nuanced than the chart suggests.

The Real Math: What You Can Actually Build

Let's run some honest numbers — not cherry-picked to make you feel either great or terrible, just realistic.

Suppose you're 45 years old, you have $15,000 in a 401(k) from a job you left years ago, and you're starting from roughly scratch. You plan to retire at 67. That gives you 22 years.

If you can contribute $800 a month — about $9,600 a year — and earn an average annual return of 7% (a conservative estimate for a diversified stock index portfolio), you'll end up with approximately $580,000. Add Social Security income — we'll cover this in detail in Chapter 7 — and you're looking at a meaningful retirement income.

Bump that contribution to $1,200 a month and the number climbs to around $870,000. If you're over 50, you get access to catch-up contributions that let you put even more into tax-advantaged accounts — we'll dig into those in Chapter 6.

The point isn't that these numbers are guaranteed. The point is that they're achievable. People hit these targets every year. Not by starting at 22 — by starting late and staying consistent.

Now let's look at someone starting even later. At 55, with zero savings and retirement at 67, you have 12 years. Contribute $1,500 a month at 7% returns and you'll have roughly $310,000. That's not a Caribbean retirement, but combined with Social Security, it can support a modest and dignified one — especially if you've paid off your home.

The shame narrative says these numbers are failures. The honest narrative says: these are real outcomes for real people who made real choices, and they are workable.

Consider Patricia, a 52-year-old hospital administrator in Cleveland. She'd worked her whole adult life in healthcare, raising two kids on her own after a divorce in her early 40s wiped out the modest retirement savings she'd built. At 52 she had $22,000 in a 403(b) and a lot of anxiety. She committed to contributing $1,400 per month — a stretch, but achievable after her daughter finished college — and reached her 65th birthday with just over $550,000. Combined with Social Security of approximately $2,100 per month, she retired comfortably. Not lavishly. Comfortably. The story that shame told her — that she'd permanently ruined her retirement — was simply false.

Why the "You Should Have Started Earlier" Conversation Is Useless

There's a particular breed of financial advice that loves to tell you what you should have done fifteen years ago. Save more in your 20s. Avoid credit card debt. Don't cash out your 401(k) when you changed jobs. Max out your IRA every year.

All of that advice is correct. It's also completely useless to you right now.

You cannot go back. The money you should have saved in 2010 is not coming back. The compound growth you missed from 2005 to 2015 is gone. Spending mental energy on that is like a doctor telling a 50-year-old patient, "You really should have started eating better in your 30s." Probably true. Absolutely not helpful.

What is helpful is understanding why many people didn't save earlier — not to excuse it, but to stop the shame spiral that prevents action today.

The real reasons people start late are almost never laziness or irresponsibility. They are:

Structural income gaps. Wages for many workers, especially those without college degrees, have stagnated for decades in real terms. When you're living paycheck to paycheck, investing feels like something that happens to other people.

Medical crises. One serious illness, one major surgery, one loved one who needed caregiving — these can wipe out years of savings and create years of debt.

Family obligations. Supporting children, aging parents, or siblings in need doesn't show up in the compound interest chart. It shows up in the real lives of real people.

Financial illiteracy by design. Personal finance is not taught in most schools. Many people arrive at adulthood genuinely not knowing how a 401(k) works, what an index fund is, or why compound interest matters. This isn't a character flaw — it's a systemic gap.

Divorce. A marital split doesn't just divide assets; it often leaves one or both partners starting over financially in their 40s or 50s. This is staggeringly common.

Bad advice or bad luck. Some people were given terrible financial guidance. Others invested in things that collapsed. Others simply ran out of runway before they figured out what they were doing.

Understanding your specific story matters — not to wallow in it, but because you need to know where you're starting from before you can plan where you're going.

The Advantage Nobody Talks About: You Know More Now

Here's something the compound interest chart will never show you: the value of experience.

A 25-year-old investor is making decisions with very limited real-world data. They've never lived through a major market crash. They've never had to choose between paying rent and funding their IRA. They've never seen a "hot" investment tip go to zero. They're making choices based on theory and optimism.

You've lived through things. You know what a real financial emergency feels like. You know which expenses you can actually cut and which ones you only think you can cut. You know your own risk tolerance in a way that only experience can teach — not as a number on a questionnaire, but as a gut-level sense of what you can actually handle.

That knowledge is worth something. The 25-year-old with a 40-year runway will often blow a significant chunk of it on mistakes that experience would have prevented: panic-selling during a crash, chasing returns into overvalued sectors, keeping lifestyle inflation perfectly in step with income growth, taking on too much risk early because the upside looked exciting.

Late starters tend to be more purposeful. They've stopped waiting for "the right time" — they know it never comes. They've stopped thinking retirement is a distant abstraction — they can feel it approaching. That urgency, properly channeled, is a genuine competitive advantage.

There's also the matter of income. A late starter who has spent two decades developing expertise and professional relationships is typically earning more than they did at 30. The person who couldn't afford to put $100 a month aside at 29 can often afford to put $1,500 a month aside at 49. The earning power that comes with experience and career progression is, in purely mechanical terms, a significant boost to late-start investing.

Debunking the Most Damaging Myths

Before moving forward, let's name the myths that are most likely to derail late starters — and dismantle them directly.

Myth 1: "It's too late to make a meaningful difference."

The math doesn't support this. Fifteen years of aggressive saving can build a portfolio that meaningfully supports retirement, especially when combined with Social Security, housing equity, and strategic timing decisions. "Too late" is almost never accurate for someone who still has more than a decade before retirement.

Myth 2: "I'd need to save so much that it's impossible."

This confuses "catching up entirely" with "making the situation substantially better." You don't need to arrive at retirement with the portfolio of someone who saved steadily for 40 years. You need enough to fill the gap between your guaranteed income and your actual expenses. That number is often smaller than people assume.

Myth 3: "The market is too risky for someone my age."

This is a misapplication of the risk-reduction-over-time principle. Yes, you should gradually shift toward a more conservative allocation as you approach retirement. But at 45, with 22 years before retirement, you still have substantial time for the market to work in your favor. Being too conservative too early is its own form of risk — inflation risk, longevity risk, the risk that your money doesn't grow enough to support you.

Myth 4: "I should focus on paying off debt before I can even think about investing."

Sometimes true, sometimes not. The debt-vs-invest question has a framework — we cover it thoroughly in Chapter 3 — but the automatic assumption that all debt must be eliminated before investing begins is often wrong and often very costly, particularly if it means missing years of employer match contributions.

Myth 5: "I'm too old to take financial risks."

Age 50 is not old in the context of a retirement plan that may need to last until age 90. The planning horizon for a 50-year-old is 40 years. That's longer than many people's entire careers. Treating that as a short time horizon and investing accordingly can be a serious mistake.

What This Book Is Actually About

This book isn't going to pretend that starting at 45 is the same as starting at 25. It isn't. Time matters. But time isn't the only variable that matters, and a late start doesn't sentence you to a bad outcome.

What this book will do is give you a clear, practical, honest path from wherever you are right now to the best version of your retirement situation — using the tools available to you, the income you actually have, and the time you realistically have left.

In the chapters ahead, we'll look at your complete financial picture without flinching (Chapter 2), work through the debt-versus-investing question that trips up so many late starters (Chapter 3), demystify the account types that give you the biggest tax advantages (Chapters 4 and 6), break down investing in plain language (Chapter 5), decode Social Security (Chapter 7), look honestly at housing and healthcare costs (Chapters 8 and 9), explore working longer as a deliberate strategy (Chapter 10), and finally, put together an actual plan with real numbers (Chapter 11).

The goal isn't to make you feel better about the past. The goal is to make the future as strong as it can possibly be — starting from today.

Because the only bad time to start is never.

Action Steps

Write down the single biggest reason you didn't start investing earlier. Not to feel bad about it — to name it clearly and put it behind you. Once it's on paper, it loses some of its power.

Search for your current or most recent employer's 401(k) plan information. If you're not enrolled, find out how to enroll. If you are enrolled, find out your current contribution percentage and what your employer matches.

Look up your Social Security projected benefit at ssa.gov/myaccount. This number — even if it's lower than you hoped — is a real asset. Knowing it is essential for planning.

Calculate your current age and your target retirement age. Write down the number of years you have. Not to panic — but to get concrete. "Someday" becomes real when it has a number attached.

Make a decision right now: commit to finishing this book before making any financial changes. You don't need to act immediately — you need to understand the full picture first. Rushing into action before you have a plan is one of the most common late-starter mistakes.

The Late-Start Success Stories Nobody Tells

Personal finance media tends to celebrate the early starters. The 30-year-old with $500,000 in retirement savings. The couple who retired at 45 through extreme frugality. These stories are real, and they're genuinely motivating for people in those situations. But they crowd out a different kind of success story that's equally real and more relevant to many readers.

The late-start success story looks like this:

Frank worked in construction for 25 years and never thought much about retirement accounts. At 52, a conversation with his daughter — who had just started her first job and was asking questions about her 401(k) — made him realize he'd never enrolled in his union's retirement plan. He had $8,000 in a savings account and no other retirement assets. At his daughter's urging, he enrolled immediately and began contributing 15% of his wages. At 58, his employer was acquired and he received a severance package of $34,000 — which he rolled into a new IRA rather than spending. He began consulting part-time at 65, earned $28,000 his first year, and contributed the maximum to a Solo 401(k). At 70, he retired with approximately $340,000 in retirement accounts.

Combined with his union pension of $1,400/month and Social Security of $2,300/month at 70 (delayed from 67), he has $3,700/month in guaranteed income and a portfolio that provides additional cushion. He lives comfortably. He travels twice a year to see his grandchildren. His story will never be featured in a personal finance magazine, but it's a success.

Marina, a 49-year-old nurse in Chicago, had $22,000 in a 403(b) when she finally paid off the last of the credit card debt she'd accumulated during a decade of single parenting. She increased her 403(b) contributions aggressively, using the money that had been going to minimum credit card payments. At 55, she accepted a promotion to nurse educator that came with a 20% salary increase. At 62, considering early retirement, she instead took a six-month sabbatical and returned part-time for three more years. She claimed Social Security at 67 ($2,600/month, full retirement age) and retired at 67 with $490,000 in her 403(b). Nobody would call her financial journey textbook. It worked.

These aren't outliers. They're patterns — the pattern of a real financial life that got complicated, then got serious, then got better.

Your story is still being written. The most important chapters — the ones where you actually build the retirement you need — may be the ones you're about to write.

Chapter 2: Your Financial Snapshot — Seeing Clearly Without Judgment

Most people's relationship with their own finances looks like this: a vague, uncomfortable feeling that things aren't great, a checking account balance they know more or less, a credit card or two they try not to think about too hard, and a stack of retirement statements they haven't opened in two years. They know enough to feel anxious but not enough to act.

The antidote to financial anxiety is almost never more money. It's more information.

Before you can build a plan, you need a baseline — a clear, accurate snapshot of where you stand today. Not where you wish you stood. Not the version you'd share at a dinner party. The real one, including the parts that make you wince.

This chapter is about getting that snapshot. It's not comfortable. It is necessary. And once you have it, the anxiety tends to drop — because you're no longer fighting a vague monster in the dark. You're dealing with specific numbers, and specific numbers can be addressed.

The Net Worth Statement: Your Starting Line

Net worth is the foundational number of personal finance. It's simple in concept: everything you own minus everything you owe. The result is either positive (you own more than you owe) or negative (you owe more than you own). Either way, it tells you exactly where you're starting from.

Pull out a piece of paper or open a spreadsheet. You're going to build this in two columns: assets and liabilities.

Your Assets

Assets are everything you own that has monetary value. Work through each category:

Liquid assets — money you can access quickly without penalty or loss.

Checking accounts: list current balances

Savings accounts: list current balances

Money market accounts

Cash and cash equivalents

Retirement accounts — these are not liquid in the traditional sense (there are penalties for early withdrawal before age 59½, with some exceptions), but they are assets.

401(k), 403(b), or 457 accounts — current balance, not the contributions you've made

Traditional IRA balances

Roth IRA balances

Old 401(k) accounts from previous employers (we'll talk about consolidating these later)

Investment accounts — brokerage accounts, taxable investment accounts, stocks, mutual funds held outside retirement accounts.

Real estate — your home's current market value if you own it. Don't guess — look up comparable sales in your neighborhood or check a site like Zillow or Redfin for an estimate. It won't be exact, but it'll be close enough for this exercise.

Other assets — a vehicle (use Kelley Blue Book value), a business you own, rental property, life insurance with a cash value component, valuable collectibles (only if you could actually sell them).

Add all of these up. That's your total assets.

Your Liabilities

Liabilities are everything you owe. Be thorough and honest here — this is where most people flinch.

Mortgage balance — call your lender or check your last statement. This is what you currently owe, not your original loan amount.

Home equity loan or HELOC — if you have one, list the outstanding balance.

Auto loans — outstanding balances on any vehicle loans.

Student loans — federal and private, all of them. Check studentaid.gov for federal loan details.

Credit cards — the total outstanding balance on each card, not the credit limit. If you're not sure, log in and check.

Personal loans — money owed to banks, credit unions, or individuals.

Medical debt — bills in collections or on payment plans.

Any other debt — IRS payment plans, back taxes, payday loans.

Add all of these up. That's your total liabilities.

Net worth = Total Assets - Total Liabilities

What the Number Means

If your net worth is positive, that's a foundation to build on. If it's negative, that's useful information — not a verdict on your worth as a person, but a clear signal about where attention needs to go first.

Take a moment to note how you feel looking at this number. Whatever comes up — relief, shame, surprise, anger — is normal. Let it land. Then set it aside, because now you're going to use the number.

Your Income and Expense Picture

Net worth tells you where you are. Income and expenses tell you how fast you're moving, and in which direction.

Track Your Income

List all sources of income on a monthly basis:

Primary job (take-home pay, not gross)

Secondary job or side income

Rental income

Child support or alimony received

Any regular investment income (dividends, etc.)

Total monthly take-home income: $________

Track Your Expenses

This is the part most people dread, but it's not as painful as it sounds if you approach it systematically.

Pull up your last three months of bank statements and credit card statements. Categorize every transaction. Most banks and credit card apps will do much of this for you automatically. What you're looking for is:

Fixed expenses — the same every month:

Rent or mortgage payment

Car payments

Insurance premiums (health, auto, home/renters, life)

Loan minimums (student loans, personal loans)

Subscriptions (gym, streaming, software)

Variable expenses — change month to month but are regular:

Groceries

Gas and transportation

Utilities

Dining out

Clothing

Entertainment

Irregular expenses — don't happen monthly but need to be accounted for:

Annual insurance payments (divide by 12)

Car maintenance and registration (divide by 12)

Home repairs and maintenance (estimate 1-2% of home value per year, divide by 12)

Medical copays and prescriptions

Gifts and holidays (estimate annual spending, divide by 12)

Add them all up. This is your actual monthly spending.

Total monthly expenses: $________

Monthly surplus (or deficit) = Income – Expenses

If the surplus is positive, that's your raw material for investing. If it's negative, the priority before anything else is closing that gap — because you can't invest money you don't have.

The Psychology of Seeing Your Numbers

Something shifts when you write these numbers down — and it's worth naming, because that shift is part of what makes this exercise valuable.

Most people carry their financial situation as a cloud of anxiety. It's there, vague and heavy, informing decisions (avoidance decisions, mostly) without ever taking a specific shape. When you convert that cloud into actual numbers, something interesting happens: the anxiety gets specific, and specific anxiety is workable in a way that vague dread is not.

"I'm in terrible financial shape" is a feeling. "I have $42,000 in net worth, $8,400 in credit card debt at 19%, and a monthly surplus of $320" is information. Information can be acted on.

Karen is a 48-year-old middle school teacher who spent three years avoiding her finances after a divorce left her with joint debts she'd had to absorb alone. When she finally sat down and did the net worth exercise from this chapter, she discovered something she hadn't expected: she had $34,000 in a 403(b) that she'd forgotten existed and $21,000 in home equity. Her situation wasn't what she'd imagined in her worst moments. It wasn't great, but it was real — and real she could work with.

The shame around money is almost always worse than the money itself. The act of looking clearly is its own form of courage, and it's the prerequisite for everything that comes next.

The Four Levers of Late-Start Wealth Building

Here's the honest truth: there are only four ways to improve your financial trajectory, and they work in combination.

Lever 1: Increase Income

This is often the highest-impact lever for late starters, and also the one that gets the least attention in traditional personal finance advice. Cutting your Netflix subscription saves you $18 a month. A raise, a career pivot, a well-chosen side project, or a promotion can add hundreds or thousands per month. We'll look at strategic income growth in Chapter 10.

For late starters, the income lever is particularly powerful because earning capacity tends to peak in the 40s and 50s. This is precisely the window when aggressive income growth, if achieved, has the maximum impact on retirement readiness.

Lever 2: Reduce Expenses

Not by suffering, but by auditing. Most people have significant spending on things they either don't need, don't notice, or wouldn't actively choose if they were paying attention. The goal is to identify that spending — not to punish yourself, but to redirect it toward your future.

Common categories where late starters consistently find recoverable money: subscriptions they've forgotten about, dining expenses that grew gradually without notice, housing costs that no longer match their actual needs, and insurance premiums that haven't been reviewed or shopped in years.

Lever 3: Reduce Debt

Debt has a cost — an interest rate that is, in effect, a guaranteed negative return on your money. High-interest debt especially is mathematically devastating to wealth building. Chapter 3 goes deep on the debt-versus-investing question.

Eliminating a $10,000 credit card balance at 22% interest is the equivalent of earning a guaranteed 22% return on that money — a return no investment can reliably match. The order in which you address debt matters, and we'll work through that framework carefully.

Lever 4: Invest More Efficiently

This means using the right accounts, minimizing fees, and letting the market do its work without interference. Chapters 4 through 6 cover this in detail.

Most late-start success stories involve pulling all four levers simultaneously, even if the movement on each is modest.

Common Financial Patterns for Late Starters

Every financial situation is unique, but certain patterns show up repeatedly among people who come to investing later in life. Recognizing yours can help you apply the right strategies.

Pattern A: The Stable Earner with No Savings

Decent income, reasonable lifestyle, but somehow nothing has accumulated. Often the culprit is lifestyle creep — expenses rose to match income over the years — combined with never automating savings. The fix is usually mechanical: automate investments before the money hits your checking account and it disappears. People in this pattern are often shocked by how much they can redirect once they actually track their spending.

Pattern B: The Recovering Debtor

Substantial consumer debt — credit cards, personal loans, maybe some medical bills — but income is workable and improving. The psychological weight of debt has made investing feel pointless ("why save when I owe so much?"). The strategy here is usually a structured debt payoff plan combined with at least minimal 401(k) contributions to capture any employer match.

Pattern C: The Interrupted Saver

Started on the right track, built some savings, then got derailed by a life event — divorce, medical crisis, job loss, business failure. May have cashed out a 401(k) during a crisis. Starting over but not actually starting from zero in terms of knowledge.

The strategy focuses on rebuilding the foundation quickly, using higher income than they had in earlier years.

Pattern D: The High Earner, Late Bloomer

Didn't earn significant income until their 40s — doctors, lawyers, business owners who went through long education or building periods. Income is now strong but retirement savings are behind where they "should" be for their age. Advantage: can invest aggressively. Strategy focuses on maxing every available account and potentially considering taxable brokerage investing.

Pattern E: The Gig Worker or Self-Employed

No employer-sponsored retirement plan, irregular income, often no benefits. May have never thought of themselves as someone who could invest because they never had a HR department telling them to sign up for a 401(k). Specific account types (Solo 401(k), SEP-IRA) are designed for exactly this situation — Chapter 4 covers them in detail.

Building Your Personal Financial Dashboard

Once you've done the net worth calculation and mapped your income and expenses, you have everything you need to build a simple financial dashboard — a one-page document you'll update quarterly.

It doesn't need to be fancy. A spreadsheet or even a handwritten page works. Include:

Date of snapshot

Total assets (broken into liquid, retirement, real estate, other)

Total liabilities (broken into mortgage, consumer debt, student loans, other)

Net worth

Monthly income

Monthly expenses

Monthly surplus

Current monthly investment contribution

Retirement account total

Review this every three months. Over time, you'll see your net worth trending upward, your liabilities shrinking, and your investment balance growing. That trend line — not the starting number — is what you're managing.

This quarterly review habit is one of the most important practices you can build. Financial progress is slow enough that you don't feel it month to month — it's visible in three-month snapshots. Quarterly tracking turns vague hope into visible evidence of progress, which makes the next three months of consistent behavior much easier.

The people who succeed at late-start wealth building aren't necessarily the ones with the best starting position. They're the ones who look clearly, make a plan, and track their progress. Clarity is what creates momentum.

Finding Money You Didn't Know You Had

One consistent finding in personal finance coaching is that most people have more financial room than they think – it's just allocated inefficiently, invisibly, or through inertia.

Consider these common sources of recoverable money that don't require lifestyle deprivation:

Refinancing existing debt. If you have a mortgage, car loan, or personal loans at interest rates above current market rates, refinancing can reduce monthly costs immediately. On a $250,000 mortgage, moving from a 7.5% to a 6% rate saves approximately $230 per month – money that can be redirected to investing without any lifestyle change.

Insurance shopping. Auto and homeowner's insurance are widely underpriced by people who haven't shopped in years. Spending two hours getting comparison quotes every three years commonly saves $300-$600 per year.

Subscription audit. The average American household spends significantly more on subscriptions than they realize, because subscriptions accumulate gradually and often aren't noticed on bank statements. A thorough review commonly surfaces $50-$150 per month in services that are no longer actively used.

Tax withholding adjustment. If you receive a large federal tax refund each year, you're giving the government an interest-free loan. Adjusting your W-4 to reduce withholding redirects that money to your paycheck – where you can invest it immediately. A $3,600 annual refund represents $300 per month you could have been investing.

None of these require spending less on anything you actually care about. They're efficiency improvements that redirect money from inefficient uses toward your retirement.

Action Steps

Complete your net worth statement today — assets minus liabilities. Use your bank and brokerage statements for exact numbers. It doesn't need to be perfect; it needs to be honest.

Pull three months of bank and credit card statements and categorize your spending. Most banking apps will do this automatically. Look for the three largest discretionary categories — that's where you have the most room to redirect money.

Calculate your monthly surplus or deficit (income minus expenses). If it's a deficit, write down one specific, concrete change you'll make this month to reduce it.

Identify your financial pattern from the five types described above. Knowing your pattern helps you apply the right strategies rather than generic advice designed for someone in a different situation.

Create your financial dashboard — even a simple spreadsheet with current date, net worth, and monthly surplus. Schedule a quarterly reminder to update it. Progress tracking is what turns intentions into momentum.

Common Net Worth Surprises (And What to Do About Them)

When people complete their first honest net worth statement, a few patterns emerge regularly. You may recognize yourself in one of them.

Surprise 1: "My net worth is actually higher than I thought." This happens when people have been mentally discounting assets — the 401(k) they haven't checked in years, home equity they hadn't thought to count, a life insurance policy with cash value, an old IRA from a job they left in 2012. If this is you, the revelation is energizing. You have more of a foundation than you realized.

Surprise 2: "My net worth is much lower than I thought." This happens when the liabilities are counted honestly for the first time — the credit card balances that felt manageable but add up to $32,000, the home equity that's been consumed by a second mortgage, the student loans that have been in deferment and quietly accumulating interest. If this is you, the discomfort is acute, but the information is precisely what you need. You cannot fix what you cannot see clearly.

Surprise 3: "I'm worth way more on paper than I feel." Homeowners sometimes discover their net worth is substantial — primarily because of home equity — while their cash situation is genuinely tight. High net worth, low liquidity. This pattern often needs addressing: significant home equity combined with high-interest consumer debt is a situation where accessing and redeploying equity (carefully, and with a clear plan) may make financial sense.

Surprise 4: "It's negative." A negative net worth — more owed than owned — is not unusual for people in their 40s who carry significant student loan, medical, or consumer debt. It's sobering, but it's also temporary. A structured plan to reduce liabilities while building assets can move net worth from negative to positive within a few years. The starting point matters less than the trajectory.

Whatever you find, the response is the same: record it, accept it, and plan from it. The numbers don't define you. The direction you move from here does.

Chapter 3: Debt First or Invest First? Making the Right Call for Your Situation

This is the question that paralyzes more late starters than almost any other. You're carrying $18,000 in credit card debt at 22% interest. You also have no retirement savings and you're 47 years old. Should you attack the debt aggressively and then start investing? Or contribute to your 401(k) now and pay the debt off on the side?

Personal finance forums will give you confident, contradictory answers. Some will tell you that high-interest debt is mathematically equivalent to a guaranteed 22% investment return, so pay it off first, always. Others will tell you that compound interest in your 401(k) is too valuable to miss, so invest while you pay debt. Both camps have math on their side. Both are missing something.

The real answer is: it depends on your specific situation. But the framework for making that decision is actually pretty clear once you understand the variables.

The Interest Rate Math

Let's start with the pure numbers, because they do matter.

When you carry debt, you're paying interest. That interest is a guaranteed loss. When you invest, you're earning returns — but those returns are not guaranteed. The stock market has historically returned around 7% per year on average after adjusting for inflation, but that average includes years of significant gains and years of significant losses.

The general rule is this: if the interest rate on your debt is higher than what you could reasonably expect to earn investing, pay the debt first. If the interest rate is lower, investing first (or simultaneously) may make more sense.

High-interest debt (above 8-10%): Credit cards, payday loans, some personal loans. At these rates, paying off the debt is almost always the better financial move. A 20% credit card rate is a guaranteed 20% "return" when you pay it off — and you'd be hard-pressed to find a consistent investment returning that.

Medium-interest debt (5-8%): Some personal loans, older student loans, some car loans. The math here is genuinely close. Investing and paying these down simultaneously often makes sense.

Low-interest debt (below 5%): Most mortgages, many student loans with income-driven repayment, some car loans. Here, investing first is often the better move because your expected investment returns are likely higher than the interest cost.

A note on taxes: Mortgage interest is partially deductible for many filers, which effectively lowers the real cost of that debt. And investment returns in tax-advantaged accounts like a 401(k) or IRA grow without being taxed each year — which makes them even more competitive relative to debt payoff.

Consider the specific math for a common late-starter situation: $15,000 in credit card debt at 21% interest. The annual interest cost on that debt is approximately $3,150 — or $262 per month in pure interest charges that buy you nothing. Every month you carry that balance, you're effectively losing $262. Paying it off eliminates that loss permanently.

Now compare to investing the same $262 per month. At 7% annual returns over five years, that $262/month generates roughly $18,500. But the $15,000 credit card balance, left untouched for five years while earning minimum payments, would still have an outstanding balance and would have cost you approximately $15,000 in interest. The math strongly favors paying the high-interest debt first.

The Employer Match Exception

Here's the one rule that overrides almost everything else: if your employer matches 401(k) contributions and you're not contributing enough to capture the full match, you are leaving free money on the table.

Employer matches are typically structured something like this: "We match 50% of your contributions up to 6% of your salary." That means if you earn $60,000 and contribute 6% ($3,600), your employer adds $1,800. That's an immediate 50% return on your contribution – no investment on the planet can compete with that.

Even if you have high-interest credit card debt, most financial advisors agree: contribute at least enough to capture the full employer match before doing anything else with extra money. The math is that decisive.

Say you have $500 extra per month. You're trying to decide between attacking your credit card debt (at 19% interest) and contributing to your 401(k) (with a 50% match up to 6% of salary, which you haven't maxed).

If you put that $500 into the 401(k) first, you get a $250 employer match – that's a 50% return before any investment growth. Even at 19% credit card interest, the match wins in year one. Capture the match. Always.

This point can't be overstated for late starters who've spent years not enrolled in their 401(k). Every year you didn't capture the employer match is a year of free money that's gone. Starting now and capturing every dollar of match going forward is the highest-priority financial action available to most employed late starters.

The Psychological Variable the Math Ignores

Here's something that financial calculators can't measure: the weight of debt on your mental health and your ability to function.

Some people can carry $25,000 in credit card debt and stay disciplined — paying minimums, contributing to their 401(k), and not touching either impulsively. Others find that the debt is so psychologically heavy that it interferes with their ability to work, make good decisions, or stay committed to any financial plan.

If you're in the second camp, the mathematically "wrong" answer — pay off the debt first, even if the numbers slightly favor investing — may be the practically right answer. A strategy you can actually stick to beats an optimal strategy you'll abandon in month three.

Marcus, a 49-year-old middle school teacher, carried $31,000 in credit card debt accumulated over a decade of financial chaos following a divorce. A financial planner told him to invest and pay down debt simultaneously. He tried it for eight months, got confused, felt overwhelmed by tracking both, and ended up making random decisions that helped neither. Eventually he chose to pause all non-match investing and attack the debt aggressively. He paid it off in 26 months. Then he invested furiously for the next 14 years. His retirement outcome was slightly less optimal than the calculator-perfect approach — but it was dramatically better than the approach that made him give up entirely.

This isn't an argument for always paying debt first. It's an argument for knowing yourself honestly. The best financial strategy is the one you'll actually follow consistently.

Debt Payoff Methods: Avalanche vs. Snowball

Once you've decided to address debt — whether exclusively or alongside investing — you need a method. Two approaches dominate.

The Avalanche Method: List your debts by interest rate from highest to lowest. Make minimum payments on all of them, then throw every extra dollar at the highest-rate debt until it's gone. Then redirect that payment to the next-highest rate, and so on. This method minimizes the total interest you pay and gets you out of debt fastest in pure mathematical terms.

For someone with three debts — a credit card at 22%, a car loan at 7%, and a personal loan at 11% — the avalanche would attack the credit card first, then the personal loan, then the car.

The Snowball Method: List your debts by balance from smallest to largest. Make minimums on all, throw everything extra at the smallest balance. When it's paid off, the full payment rolls to the next-smallest. The psychology here is momentum: each debt paid off is a genuine win that reinforces the behavior.

The avalanche saves more money. The snowball keeps more people on track. Research on debt payoff behavior consistently shows that people who start with their smallest balance are more likely to pay off all their debt than those who start with their highest-rate balance, even though the latter saves more money. Choose based on what you know about yourself.

A hybrid approach works for some people: start with the snowball (one or two small wins to build confidence and prove the system works), then switch to the avalanche once you have momentum.

A Practical Framework: The Priority Stack

Here's the order of operations that makes sense for most late starters. It's not a rigid law — it's a decision framework. Adjust it based on your interest rates and your situation.

Step 1: Build a minimal emergency fund

Before aggressively paying debt or investing, make sure you have at least $1,000-$2,000 liquid in a savings account. Without this, the first unexpected expense forces you to run up more credit card debt, undoing your progress. Three-to-six months of expenses is the traditional target; get to $1,000-$2,000 first and then build from there.

Step 2: Capture the full employer match

Contribute enough to your 401(k) to get every dollar of employer match. This comes before extra debt payments, before IRA contributions, before everything except the emergency fund floor.

Step 3: Pay off high-interest debt (above 10%)

Throw everything you can spare at your highest-interest debt using the avalanche method (highest interest rate first) or the snowball method (smallest balance first for psychological wins). The avalanche method saves more money; the snowball method keeps more people on track. Choose based on what works for you.

Step 4: Build emergency fund to 3-6 months of expenses

Now that high-interest debt is gone, fully fund your emergency reserve before investing aggressively. This protects you from having to take on new debt when life happens.

Step 5: Max tax-advantaged retirement accounts

After high-interest debt is gone and emergency fund is built, direct as much as possible into your 401(k) (beyond the match), IRA, or Roth IRA. These accounts give you tax advantages that regular brokerage accounts don't — we'll cover this in detail in Chapter 4.

Step 6: Pay off medium-interest debt (5-10%)

Credit cards should already be gone. This step usually covers car loans, some student loans, and personal loans in the 5-10% range. You can do this simultaneously with Step 5.

Step 7: Invest in taxable brokerage accounts

Once you've maxed your tax-advantaged accounts, low-interest debt remaining (like a 3% mortgage), and want to invest more, taxable brokerage accounts are your next option.

Step 8: Pay off low-interest debt

Only at this point does accelerating your mortgage payoff make mathematical sense — and even then, it's a personal decision, not always the optimal financial move.

Debt Types That Need Special Attention

Not all debt is the same, and some types deserve individual consideration.

Student Loans

Federal student loans come with options that private debt doesn't offer: income-driven repayment plans, potential forgiveness programs (especially for public service workers), and the possibility of deferment during financial hardship.

If you have significant federal student loan debt, your first call should be to studentaid.gov to understand your options before throwing extra money at these loans. Many late starters discover that income-driven repayment dramatically lowers their required monthly payment, freeing up money for retirement investing — and that after 20-25 years (or 10 years for PSLF), remaining balances can be forgiven.

Private student loans don't come with these protections. Treat them more like personal loans, and factor their interest rate into your priority stack.

Medical Debt

Medical debt is often negotiable in ways that other debt is not. Hospitals frequently offer payment plans with zero interest, and many will reduce the total amount owed if you negotiate directly or request financial assistance. Before making large payments on medical debt, call the provider's billing department and ask about hardship programs and negotiated settlements.

Medical debt under $500 was removed from credit reports in 2023, and debt under $2,500 was removed in 2025 — which reduces the credit impact of this debt category significantly.

Car Loans

The question with car loans isn't usually "pay it off or invest?" — it's whether you should own the car you do. If your car payment is consuming 15% of your take-home income, that's a structural problem. Depending on how much you owe versus what the car is worth, selling and buying something cheaper with cash (or a much smaller loan) can free up hundreds per month for investing. The math often works in your favor, especially if the loan carries a mid-range interest rate.

What to Do When the Debt Feels Insurmountable

Some people reading this chapter aren't dealing with $8,000 in credit card debt. They're dealing with $75,000, or more — a combination of credit cards, medical bills, personal loans, and old debts in collections. The priority stack above assumes the debt is manageable. When it isn't, different tools apply.

Nonprofit credit counseling: Organizations like the National Foundation for Credit Counseling (NFCC) offer free or low-cost debt management plans that can consolidate multiple credit card payments into a single monthly payment with reduced interest rates. This is different from debt settlement (which damages your credit) and from for-profit credit counseling companies (which are often predatory).

Bankruptcy: A difficult conversation, but sometimes the right one. Chapter 7 bankruptcy can discharge unsecured debt and reset your financial life. Chapter 13 sets up a court-supervised repayment plan. Either option has significant long-term credit implications, but for some people — particularly those whose debt genuinely exceeds any realistic ability to repay — it represents a viable path to a fresh start. A consultation with a bankruptcy attorney (many offer free initial consultations) can clarify whether this is worth considering.

Debt consolidation loans: If you can qualify for a personal loan at a substantially lower interest rate than your credit cards, consolidating high-interest debt can reduce your monthly interest cost and simplify repayment. Be cautious here: consolidation only helps if you stop adding new debt, and many people consolidate and then run the credit cards back up.

Debt settlement: A last resort before bankruptcy. You negotiate with creditors to pay less than the full balance in exchange for settling the account. This damages your credit significantly, may have tax implications (forgiven debt is often treated as taxable income), and should only be considered when the alternative is bankruptcy. Use it deliberately, not impulsively.

The goal of this chapter isn't to give you a one-size answer — it's to give you a framework so that whatever you decide, you're deciding with clear information rather than vague anxiety.

Making Peace with "Imperfect" Progress

One final mindset note: the debt-vs-invest decision rarely has a clean, unambiguous right answer. The numbers favor one choice, your psychology favors another, your specific debt types add complexity, and your financial situation will change over the next several years in ways you can't fully anticipate.

What matters more than getting the optimization perfect is choosing a path and following it consistently. A plan that is 90% optimal and consistently executed beats a theoretically perfect plan that you second-guess, adjust, abandon, and restart every few months.

Make the best decision you can with the information in this chapter. Execute it. Revisit it in six months. Adjust based on results. That's not settling — that's how financial progress actually works in real life.

Action Steps

List every debt you have: balance, interest rate, and minimum monthly payment. Organize them by interest rate from highest to lowest. This is your debt inventory.

Check your 401(k) employer match details. Log into your benefits portal or call HR. Confirm exactly what percentage you need to contribute to capture the full match, and verify that you're currently contributing at least that much.

Calculate the interest you're paying monthly on your highest-rate debt. If you have a $10,000 credit card at 22%, that's roughly $183 in interest every month — money that buys you nothing. Seeing that number concretely often changes how urgent payoff feels.

Choose your debt payoff method: avalanche (highest interest first, saves the most money) or snowball (smallest balance first, builds momentum). There's no wrong answer — the right method is the one you'll actually stick to.

If you have federal student loans, log into studentaid.gov and review your current repayment plan. Compare your current monthly payment against what an income-driven repayment plan would cost. If there's a significant gap, the difference might be money better directed toward retirement investing.

The Emergency Fund as Debt Prevention

One aspect of the debt-versus-invest discussion that doesn't get enough attention is the emergency fund's role as a debt firewall. Many late starters who struggle with credit card debt aren't in debt because they overspend on luxuries — they're in debt because every emergency sends them to a credit card.

The refrigerator breaks: $800 on the credit card. The car needs brakes: $700. A health issue requires a specialist copay: $450 that shouldn't have to be financed but is.

Without an emergency fund, these completely normal life events become debt events. And each debt event adds to the balance that's accruing at 22% interest. The emergency fund doesn't just provide peace of mind — it breaks the debt cycle at the point where new debt would enter the system.

For a late starter with existing credit card debt, this creates a sequencing dilemma: if you use all your spare cash to pay off the credit card, you have no emergency fund. The next emergency sends the card right back up. If you build the emergency fund first while the credit card accrues interest, you're paying more in interest.

The practical answer most financial advisors land on: build a small emergency fund ($1,000-$2,000) first, then attack the credit card debt aggressively, then replenish the emergency fund to 3-6 months once the high-interest debt is gone. The small starter emergency fund prevents the most common debt relapses while keeping the debt payoff timeline aggressive.

The psychological value of this approach is also real. Knowing you have $1,500 accessible for genuine emergencies changes your relationship to the debt payoff process. It becomes something you're choosing to do rather than something you're forced to do, with nothing to protect you if anything goes wrong.

Debt and Relationships

Money conversations between partners are among the most conflict-laden in relationships, and debt is particularly fraught. If you're working through a debt situation while in a relationship, the process of getting clear and making a plan extends to a shared financial picture.

In dual-income households, aligning on the priority stack is essential. One partner who is attacking debt aggressively while the other continues spending freely will make no progress. One partner who wants to invest for the future while the other is focused on eliminating debt first can lead to resentment and conflict over resource allocation.

A shared budget conversation — ideally using the net worth snapshot and expense tracking from Chapter 2 as the foundation — and a shared agreement on the priority stack is the infrastructure that makes couple financial planning work. It doesn't need to be perfect agreement on every detail. It needs to be enough shared direction that both people's behavior moves the household toward the same goals.

For couples where one partner has significantly more debt than the other — perhaps from before the relationship, from a previous marriage, or from a period of solo income — the question of "whose debt is it" can be emotionally complicated. Legally in most states, debt incurred before marriage remains the individual's responsibility. Practically, whether you treat it as "your debt" or "our debt" is a relationship decision, not just a financial one. What matters most is having the conversation explicitly rather than letting assumptions and resentment accumulate around it.

Chapter 4: The Accounts You Need — 401(k), IRA, Roth, and What Actually Makes Sense for You

Walk into a financial planning conversation and you'll hear alphabet soup within the first five minutes: 401(k), 403(b), IRA, Roth, HSA, SEP-IRA, SIMPLE IRA, Solo 401(k). Most people tune out around the third acronym, nod politely, and leave more confused than when they arrived.

That's a problem, because the specific accounts you use for retirement saving matter more than most people realize. Two people earning the same income, saving the same amount, and investing in the exact same funds can end up with dramatically different outcomes in retirement depending on whether they used the right account types. The tax advantages embedded in these accounts are one of the most powerful tools available to late starters — but only if you understand them well enough to use them.

This chapter will cut through the jargon and give you a clear picture of what each account type does, who it's for, and how to choose.

Why Account Type Matters: The Tax Question

Every investment account has a tax treatment. Understanding three categories covers the vast majority of what you'll encounter:

Tax-deferred accounts: You contribute pre-tax money. You don't pay income tax on contributions in the year you make them. Your investments grow without being taxed each year. You pay income tax when you withdraw the money in retirement. Examples: Traditional 401(k), Traditional IRA.

Tax-free accounts: You contribute after-tax money — you've already paid income tax on it. Your investments grow without being taxed. You pay no tax when you withdraw in retirement (assuming you follow the rules). Examples: Roth 401(k), Roth IRA.

Taxable accounts: No special tax treatment. You invest after-tax money, pay taxes on dividends and capital gains each year, and pay capital gains taxes when you sell. These are standard brokerage accounts — useful after you've maxed tax-advantaged options.

The difference between these can be enormous over time. An investment that grows from $10,000 to $100,000 inside a tax-deferred account doesn't generate a single dollar of tax along the way. In a taxable account, you'd pay taxes on every dividend along the path. That friction compounds, and over decades it can cost tens of thousands of dollars in lost wealth.

To put real numbers on this: consider a $50,000 investment growing at 7% annually for 20 years. In a tax-advantaged account, it grows to approximately $193,000, all available for spending (with taxes on withdrawal for Traditional accounts). In a taxable account with a 25% blended tax rate on gains along the way, the actual take-home would be closer to $155,000. The difference — $38,000 — is the value of the tax advantage, and it comes purely from using the right account type, not from different investments or higher returns.

The 401(k): Your First Stop (If You Have an Employer)

A 401(k) is a retirement account sponsored by your employer. It's named after the section of the IRS code that created it — which tells you something about how exciting financial regulators are at naming things.

Here's how it works: You tell your employer what percentage of your paycheck to direct into your 401(k) before taxes are withheld. That money goes into your account and gets invested — typically in a menu of mutual funds chosen by your employer's plan administrator. Your taxable income is reduced by your contribution amount, so you pay less income tax in the year you contribute.

2025 contribution limits for 401(k):

Under 50: $23,500 per year

50 and older: $31,000 per year (the extra $7,500 is the "catch-up contribution" — more on this in Chapter 6)

Many employers offer a match — they'll contribute additional money based on what you contribute, up to a limit. As we discussed in Chapter 3, this match is the highest-return financial move available to you. Use it.

Traditional vs. Roth 401(k): Many plans now offer both options within the same 401(k). The Traditional version is tax-deferred (pre-tax contributions, taxes paid on withdrawal). The Roth version is tax-free (after-tax contributions, no taxes on withdrawal). We'll discuss how to choose in a moment.

403(b) and 457 plans: These work almost identically to 401(k)s but are offered by different employer types. 403(b) plans are for nonprofit organizations, public schools, and some healthcare organizations. 457(b) plans are typically for state and local government employees. If you work in public education, healthcare, or government, you likely have one of these rather than a traditional 401(k). The mechanics — contribution limits, tax treatment, employer matching — are essentially the same.

What if your employer plan is terrible? Some 401(k) plans have genuinely terrible fund options — high-fee actively managed funds with no low-cost index fund alternatives. If that's your situation, still contribute enough to capture the full employer match, then direct additional retirement savings into an IRA (covered below), which gives you full control over your investment options.

Evaluating your 401(k) plan requires looking at the expense ratios of the available funds. Look for funds with expense ratios below 0.20%. If your cheapest option is a target-date fund at 0.15% or an S&P 500 index fund at 0.05%, great. If your only options are actively managed funds charging 1% or more, you're paying significantly for a service that statistically underperforms — and the IRA becomes your most important account after the match threshold.

The IRA: Your Individual Retirement Account

An IRA is a retirement account you open yourself, independent of any employer. You can contribute up to $7,000 per year in 2025 (under age 50) or $8,000 if you're 50 or older.

The lower limit compared to a 401(k) makes the IRA feel like a minor supplement — but it's actually powerful, especially because it gives you complete control over your investment choices. You can open an IRA at any major brokerage (Fidelity, Vanguard, Schwab) and invest in virtually any stock, bond, or fund available.

Traditional IRA: Pre-tax contributions (tax-deferred growth, taxes paid on withdrawal). Importantly, the deductibility of contributions phases out if you have access to a workplace retirement plan and your income exceeds certain thresholds. In 2025, for married couples filing jointly, deductibility phases out between $126,000 and $146,000 of modified adjusted gross income if the contributing spouse has a workplace plan.

Roth IRA: After-tax contributions, tax-free withdrawals. Eligibility phases out at higher incomes — in 2025, Roth IRA contributions phase out for single filers between $150,000 and $165,000, and for married filing jointly between $236,000 and $246,000.

The spousal IRA: If your spouse doesn't work or has very low income, they can still contribute to an IRA based on your earned income. This effectively doubles the family's IRA contribution capacity. A working spouse earning $80,000 can fully fund both their own IRA ($8,000 if 50+) and their non-working spouse's IRA ($8,000), for a combined $16,000 in annual IRA contributions.

One important rule about IRAs: you must have earned income (wages, salary, self-employment income) at least equal to your contribution. You can't contribute $8,000 to an IRA in a year when you only earned $3,000.

Traditional vs. Roth: The Decision Framework

This is one of the most common questions in retirement planning, and the answer is genuinely situational.

Choose Traditional (tax-deferred) when:

You expect to be in a lower tax bracket in retirement than you are now

You need the current-year tax deduction to make the numbers work

Your income is high enough that Roth contributions aren't an option

You expect your income to drop significantly in the years before retirement

Choose Roth (tax-free) when:

You expect to be in the same or higher tax bracket in retirement

You're currently in a lower income year (between jobs, early in a career pivot)

You want tax-free income in retirement to manage your tax bracket

Tax rates seem likely to rise in the future (uncertain, but a reasonable concern)

You want more flexibility — Roth IRAs have no required minimum distributions during your lifetime

The late-starter perspective: For many people in their 40s and 50s, a mix of both is optimal. Contributing to a Traditional 401(k) reduces current taxable income (useful when you're in your peak earning years), while also building a Roth IRA gives you tax diversification in retirement — the flexibility to draw from different account types to manage your tax bracket year by year.

Many late starters are in their highest-earning decade right now. If that's you, reducing your current tax bill via Traditional pre-tax contributions is genuinely valuable. At the same time, if you can also fund a Roth account, the tax-free growth there is a long-term asset.

Consider how this plays out in practice: a 52-year-old earning $90,000 who contributes $20,000 to a Traditional 401(k) reduces their federal taxable income to $70,000. At a 22% marginal rate, that's $4,400 saved in taxes this year — money that stays in their pocket. Meanwhile, a separately funded Roth IRA (up to $8,000 at 52) provides a pool of money that will never be taxed again. The combination covers both present (tax reduction) and future (tax-free income) financial goals.

Accounts for the Self-Employed

If you're a freelancer, contractor, business owner, or otherwise self-employed, you don't have access to an employer 401(k) — but you have access to several account types specifically designed for you, and some of them have dramatically higher contribution limits.

SEP-IRA (Simplified Employee Pension IRA):

Contribution limit in 2025: up to 25% of net self-employment income, maximum $70,000

Easy to set up — available at any major brokerage

Contributions are tax-deductible (Traditional treatment only — no Roth option)

No catch-up contributions for those over 50

Ideal for: freelancers and solo business owners who want simplicity and high contribution limits

If you earned $100,000 net from self-employment, you could contribute up to $25,000 to a SEP-IRA. That's significantly more than the $23,500 limit on a standard 401(k).

Solo 401(k) (also called Individual 401(k) or Self-Employed 401(k)):

Contribution limit in 2025: up to $69,000 total, combining employee contributions ($23,500, or $31,000 if 50+) and employer contributions (25% of net self-employment income)

More complex to set up than a SEP-IRA, but more powerful

Can have a Roth component (check with your brokerage — not all offer it)

Catch-up contributions available for those 50+

Ideal for: self-employed individuals who want to maximize contributions and have the income to support them

Consider a self-employed consultant earning $120,000 net. With a Solo 401(k) at age 55, she could contribute $31,000 as the "employee" portion and up to 25% of self-employment compensation (approximately $27,000 at that income level after adjustments) as the "employer" portion — for a total contribution potentially exceeding $55,000 in a single year. That's an extraordinary catch-up mechanism available almost exclusively to the self-employed.

SIMPLE IRA:

Designed for small businesses with employees (up to 100)

Contribution limit: $16,500 in 2025 ($20,000 for those 50+)

Less common for solo self-employed individuals but worth knowing about if you run a small business with a handful of employees

Health Savings Accounts: The Hidden Retirement Account

The Health Savings Account (HSA) isn't labeled a retirement account, but it functions as one — and for late starters with access to one, it's extraordinarily valuable.

HSAs are available if you have a High Deductible Health Plan (HDHP). The triple tax advantage is unique in the tax code:

Contributions are tax-deductible (or pre-tax through payroll)

Growth is tax-free

Withdrawals for qualified medical expenses are tax-free

After age 65, you can withdraw for any reason — if it's not a medical expense, you pay ordinary income tax, just like a Traditional IRA. But if you use it for healthcare costs (which will be substantial in retirement — we'll explore this in Chapter 9), it's entirely tax-free.

In 2025, HSA contribution limits are $4,300 for an individual and $8,550 for a family, with an additional $1,000 catch-up for those 55+.

The optimal strategy: contribute to your HSA, invest the funds in low-cost index funds (not the default money market account), and don't touch it until retirement. Pay current medical expenses out of pocket if possible, and keep receipts —

you can reimburse yourself from the HSA years later for qualified past expenses.

Many late starters overlook the HSA because they don't have a HDHP, or because they assume it's just a way to pay current medical bills. Used strategically, a fully funded HSA could add $100,000 or more to your retirement assets over a decade – all completely tax-free when used for medical expenses.

Rolling Over Old 401(k)s

Many late starters have remnants of their working lives scattered across old employer 401(k) accounts – sometimes three or four of them. This is more common than most financial advisors acknowledge. The Department of Labor has estimated millions of unclaimed retirement accounts worth an estimated $1.65 trillion.

If you have old 401(k)s floating around at former employers, you have options:

Roll it into your current employer's 401(k): Simplest option if the current plan has good investment options.

Roll it into an IRA: Gives you the widest investment options and full control. Open a Rollover IRA at a brokerage, request a direct rollover from the old plan, and the money transfers without tax consequences.

Leave it where it is: Acceptable if the plan has good options and low fees. Not ideal – accounts with former employers can become difficult to manage and easy to forget.

Cash it out: Almost never the right answer. You'll pay ordinary income tax on the full amount plus a 10% early withdrawal penalty if you're under 59½. A $40,000 account can easily net you $24,000 after taxes and penalties. Many people have done this during a financial crisis — there's no shame in it — but if you have a choice, preserve that money.

When rolling over, always choose a direct rollover (trustee to trustee) rather than taking a check in your name. If the check comes to you, you have 60 days to redeposit it in an eligible account, and the plan is required to withhold 20% for taxes — which you'd need to come up with out of pocket to avoid a taxable distribution on that withheld amount. A direct rollover eliminates this complication entirely.

Action Steps

Confirm what retirement accounts your current employer offers. Log into your HR portal or call benefits. Verify the employer match percentage and confirm you're contributing enough to capture the full match.

Open an IRA if you don't already have one. Fidelity, Vanguard, and Charles Schwab all offer straightforward IRA accounts with no account minimums and access to low-cost index funds. The whole process takes about 20 minutes online.

Decide Traditional or Roth based on your situation. If you're in a high tax bracket now and expect lower income in retirement, lean Traditional. If you're in a moderate bracket or expect taxes to rise, lean Roth. A mix is often ideal.

If you're self-employed, research SEP-IRA and Solo 401(k) options at a major brokerage. The potential contribution limits are dramatically higher than standard 401(k)s — this is one of the most powerful tools available for self-employed late starters.

Search for any old 401(k) accounts at former employers. The National Registry of Unclaimed Retirement Benefits (unclaimedretirementbenefits.com) can help locate lost accounts. Then plan a rollover to consolidate them somewhere you can actually manage them.

The Nondeductible Traditional IRA and the Backdoor Roth

For late starters with higher incomes who exceed the Roth IRA eligibility limits, there's a strategy that allows them to effectively make Roth contributions despite the income restriction. It's called the backdoor Roth IRA.

Here's how it works:

Make a nondeductible contribution to a Traditional IRA (up to $8,000 for those 50+)

Convert that Traditional IRA to a Roth IRA shortly after contribution

Because the contribution was nondeductible (after-tax money), the conversion triggers little or no tax

The "backdoor" name reflects the indirect path to Roth eligibility. It's fully legal and explicitly endorsed by the IRS in its guidance documents.

One important caveat: if you have existing pre-tax Traditional IRA balances, the pro-rata rule applies. The IRS looks at all your Traditional IRA money (deductible and nondeductible)

together when calculating the taxable portion of any conversion. If you have $90,000 in a pre-tax IRA and make a $8,000 nondeductible contribution, only about 8% of any conversion you do is tax-free — not the full amount. For people with large existing traditional IRA balances, the backdoor Roth is more complicated and may not be worth pursuing.

The solution to the pro-rata problem: many people with traditional IRA balances roll those IRAs into their current employer's 401(k) plan (which accepts rollovers), clearing the traditional IRA to allow a clean backdoor Roth contribution. Not all 401(k) plans accept IRA rollovers, but many do — worth checking with your plan administrator.

For late starters in their 50s who are in high-income years and want to build Roth assets, understanding and potentially utilizing the backdoor Roth can meaningfully expand their options.

Protecting Your Accounts: Beneficiaries and Account Security

A practical note that often goes unaddressed: the accounts you're building need basic protective infrastructure.

Beneficiary designations revisited: As mentioned in Chapter 6, beneficiary designations on retirement accounts supersede your will. Every account — 401(k), IRA, Roth IRA — should have current, correct primary and contingent beneficiary designations. Review these when you open an account and after any major life change (marriage, divorce, death of a named beneficiary, birth of children or grandchildren).

Account security: Retirement accounts are high-value targets for identity theft and fraud. Enable two-factor authentication on every financial account that offers it. Use strong, unique passwords (a password manager makes this practical). Monitor your accounts regularly — quarterly at minimum, monthly if you're actively building assets. Sign up for alerts (email or text) for large transactions or logins from new devices.

Consolidation: Fewer accounts are easier to monitor, secure, and manage. If you've accumulated multiple IRAs at different institutions over the years, consolidating them at a single custodian simplifies your financial life and reduces the risk of losing track of an account.

Chapter 5: Investing Without an MBA — Index Funds, Asset Allocation, and the Power of Simplicity

Here is a secret that Wall Street would prefer you didn't know: most professional money managers don't beat the market over the long term. A meta-analysis of actively managed mutual funds found that after fees, roughly 80-90% of them underperform their benchmark index over a 15-year period. The managers who do outperform in a given year rarely sustain that performance — and it's nearly impossible to identify them in advance.

Meanwhile, a simple index fund sitting in a Vanguard or Fidelity account, doing nothing but tracking the market, quietly beats those professionals year after year, decade after decade.

This chapter is about the investing approach that is simultaneously the simplest and the most effective: index fund investing. It's what most evidence-based financial advisors recommend. It's what billionaire Warren Buffett recommends for regular investors. And it requires no financial expertise to implement.

What Is an Index Fund?

An index is a list of stocks or bonds that represents a market or market segment. The S&P 500 index, for example, is a list of 500 large U.S. companies — Apple, Microsoft, Amazon, JPMorgan, Procter & Gamble, and 495 others. When people say "the market was up 12% this year," they're often referring to the S&P 500.

An index fund is simply a fund that holds all the stocks in a specific index in proportion to their size. A total U.S. stock market index fund owns a tiny slice of every publicly traded U.S. company — thousands of companies, bought automatically in proportion to their market value.

The beauty of this approach:

Automatic diversification. When you buy a total market index fund, you own a piece of every major company in America. If one company tanks, it barely registers in your overall portfolio. When Enron collapsed in 2001, it was a catastrophe for people who held Enron stock directly — but holders of a total market fund experienced only a small blip, because Enron was a tiny fraction of the overall index.

Low fees. Active funds employ analysts, portfolio managers, and researchers to try to pick winning stocks. All of that costs money, reflected in the fund's expense ratio – the annual fee charged as a percentage of assets. Many actively managed funds charge 1-1.5% per year. A Vanguard or Fidelity index fund often charges 0.03-0.10% per year. On a $200,000 portfolio, that's the difference between paying $2,000-$3,000 per year in fees versus paying $60-$200. Over 20 years, the compounding impact of those fee savings is enormous.

Predictable behavior. Index funds don't make bets. They don't try to time the market. They own the market. You know exactly what you own and why.

The fee difference deserves a concrete illustration. Say you invest $150,000 and leave it for 20 years. At 7% annual return:

In a low-cost index fund (0.05% expense ratio): approximately $574,000

In a typical actively managed fund (1.1% expense ratio): approximately $465,000

The difference is nearly $110,000 – just from fees. The actively managed fund would need to outperform the index by over 1% annually, every year, for 20 years just to break even. The overwhelming majority fail to do this.

The Three-Fund Portfolio: A Remarkably Complete Solution

The three-fund portfolio is a concept popularized by the Bogleheads community (followers of Vanguard founder John Bogle's investment philosophy). It holds that you need exactly three index funds to build a globally diversified, low-cost portfolio:

Total U.S. Stock Market Index Fund — owns every publicly traded U.S. company

Total International Stock Market Index Fund — owns every major publicly traded company outside the U.S.

Total Bond Market Index Fund — owns a broad range of U.S. government and corporate bonds

That's it. Three funds cover the entire global stock and bond market. There's no need for sector funds, dividend funds, REIT funds, small-cap funds, or any other specialized product — though some investors choose to add a slice of these for personal reasons.

At Vanguard, Fidelity, and Schwab, each of these three fund types is available at extremely low cost:

Vanguard:

VTSAX / VTI (Total U.S. Stock Market)

VTIAX / VXUS (Total International)

VBTLX / BND (Total Bond Market)

Fidelity:

FSKAX / FZROX (Total U.S. Stock Market, FZROX has zero expense ratio)

FTIHX / FZILX (Total International)

FXNAX (Total Bond Market)

Schwab:

SWTSX (Total U.S. Stock Market)

SWISX or SCHF (International)

SWAGX (Total Bond Market)

Your 401(k) may not have these exact funds available. Look for funds with "index" in the name, "S&P 500" or "total market" in the description, and expense ratios below 0.20%. If the lowest-cost fund in your plan is an S&P 500 index fund, use that for the U.S. equity portion.

Asset Allocation: The Most Important Decision You'll Make

Asset allocation is the question of what percentage of your portfolio to hold in stocks versus bonds. This single decision accounts for more of your long-term investment outcome than any stock-picking or market-timing decision you could make.

Stocks have historically returned more than bonds over long periods — but they fluctuate wildly in the short term. Bonds are more stable but return less. The right mix depends on two things: your time horizon (how long before you need the money) and your risk tolerance (how much of a short-term drop you can handle without panic-selling).

The old rule of thumb: Hold your age in bonds. At 40, hold 40% bonds. At 60, hold 60% bonds. This has become outdated because people live longer and need their money to last 30+ years in retirement, not 15.

A more modern approach: Subtract your age from 120, and that's your approximate stock percentage.

Age 45: 75% stocks, 25% bonds

Age 55: 65% stocks, 35% bonds

Age 65: 55% stocks, 45% bonds

This is a starting point, not a rule. Your actual allocation should account for:

Time horizon: If you're 48 and planning to retire at 70, you have 22 years. That's long enough to be quite aggressive — you have time to recover from market downturns.

Risk tolerance: The true test of risk tolerance isn't a questionnaire — it's how you behaved in March 2020, when markets dropped 34% in five weeks. Did you stay the course? Did you panic-sell? Did you buy more? Your honest answer to that question should inform your allocation.

Other income sources: If you'll have a pension or guaranteed income that covers your basic expenses, you can afford to hold more stocks with your investment portfolio, knowing the volatility doesn't threaten your floor.

Rule of thumb for late starters: Because you need your money to grow meaningfully in the time you have, most financial advisors suggest late starters lean slightly more aggressive than their age-based allocation might suggest — perhaps 70-80% stocks through your mid-50s, shifting toward 60-65% stocks as you approach retirement.

How the Market Actually Behaves: Setting Realistic Expectations

Before you invest, you need to understand what you're agreeing to. The stock market does not go up in a steady line. It goes up dramatically over long periods, but it does so through crashes, corrections, and stretches of sideways movement that feel alarming when you're living through them.

Historical context for the U.S. stock market:

Average annual return from 1928-2023: approximately 9.8% (about 7% after inflation)

Market declines of 10% or more happen roughly every 16 months

Market declines of 20% or more (bear markets) happen roughly every 3-4 years

The average bear market lasts about 9-10 months before recovery begins

The worst drops in modern history: 1929-1932 (down 86%), 2000-2002 (down 49%), 2007-2009 (down 57%), 2020 (down 34%, recovered in 5 months)

Every single one of those crashes was followed by a recovery that reached new all-time highs. Every one. Investors who stayed invested through those declines were eventually rewarded. Investors who sold at the bottom locked in losses they never recovered.

The COVID crash of March 2020 is worth examining closely, because it offers a clear lesson. Markets fell 34% in five weeks — an extraordinarily rapid and frightening decline. Many investors sold, locking in catastrophic losses. But from the bottom of that crash in late March 2020, the S&P 500 returned over 90% in the following 12 months. Investors who stayed in their index funds didn't just recover — they thrived.

The practical implication for late starters: your biggest risk is not market volatility — it's selling during a downturn and missing the recovery. This is why understanding your allocation and knowing in advance that drops will happen is so important. You can't be surprised into panic if you were expecting the fluctuation.

A useful mental model: don't think of your account balance as "money you have." Think of it as a number that will go up and down over time, and the value of which will be determined years from now when you actually need it. On a -20% day, your retirement account doesn't have less money in the way that matters — it has the same number of fund shares, just priced temporarily lower. Those shares will be worth more later.

Dollar-Cost Averaging: Consistency Over Timing

Market timing — trying to buy when markets are low and sell when they're high — sounds logical. It has almost never worked consistently for ordinary investors, and studies consistently show that even professional fund managers fail at it the majority of the time.

Dollar-cost averaging is the alternative: investing a fixed amount on a regular schedule regardless of what the market is doing. When you contribute $500 to your 401(k) every paycheck, you're dollar-cost averaging automatically. Sometimes you're buying shares at higher prices; sometimes at lower prices. Over time, you average out.

The mathematical result: you buy more shares when prices are low (because your fixed dollar amount buys more at lower prices) and fewer when prices are high. This actually tends to reduce your average cost per share over time compared to lump-sum investing — and more importantly, it removes the psychological trap of trying to time the market.

Consider what dollar-cost averaging does during a bear market. When the market drops 30%, your regular monthly contribution buys 43% more shares than it would at the previous price. Those extra shares participate fully in the recovery. A prolonged bear market is, paradoxically, excellent news for someone who is still in the accumulation phase and contributing regularly.

For late starters, this is both the practical and the psychological right approach. Automate your contributions. Don't watch the market daily. Let the system work.

Rebalancing: Keeping Your Allocation on Track

Over time, your portfolio will drift from its target allocation. If stocks have a great year and bonds lag, you might go from a

70/30 stocks/bonds split to 80/20. That's more risk than you intended. Rebalancing brings you back to your target.

The simplest approach: rebalance once a year. Look at your portfolio in January (or whatever month you choose), see how far you've drifted, and move money from the overweighted category to the underweighted category.

Don't rebalance too frequently — transaction costs (even in low-cost accounts) and tax consequences in taxable accounts can erode the benefit. Annual rebalancing is sufficient.

If you're adding money regularly through paycheck contributions, you can also direct new contributions toward underweighted categories, which naturally rebalances without requiring you to sell.

One rebalancing strategy that works particularly well for late starters with limited time: set your new contributions to go entirely into whatever asset class is currently most underweighted. If stocks have surged and bonds are below target, direct all new contributions to the bond index fund until you're back to your target ratio. This "contribution-based rebalancing" avoids selling altogether, which eliminates both the tax complication (in taxable accounts) and the psychological difficulty of selling things that have been growing.

Common Investing Mistakes to Avoid

The investing approach described in this chapter — diversified low-cost index funds, consistent contributions, appropriate allocation, annual rebalancing — is straightforward. But simple doesn't mean easy, because the financial media, your instincts, and the behavior of other investors will work against you in specific predictable ways.

Mistake 1: Chasing last year's winners. Every year, certain sectors or funds produce exceptional returns. The following year, investors flood into them — usually just in time to experience the reversion to mean. Studies consistently show that funds at the top of performance rankings attract the most new money, and subsequent performance is usually disappointing.

Mistake 2: Panic-selling in downturns. The single most damaging behavior for long-term investors. Studies of investor behavior show that the average investor's actual returns significantly underperform the funds they're invested in — because they sell after drops and buy back after recoveries, consistently doing the opposite of what they should.

Mistake 3: Over-concentrating in employer stock. Some 401(k) plans offer company stock as an option, and some employees (out of loyalty, familiarity, or inertia) put large percentages of their retirement savings there. This concentrates risk dramatically. Enron employees who held significant employer stock in their 401(k)s lost both their jobs and their retirement savings simultaneously when the company collapsed. Diversify.

Mistake 4: Letting inertia keep you in bad funds. If your 401(k) was automatically enrolled you into an expensive balanced fund several years ago and you've never looked at it, you may be paying 0.8% or more when a better option exists within the same plan. Checking and optimizing your fund selection once when you read this chapter can save significant money over time.

Mistake 5: Waiting for the "right time." Studies have shown that even perfect market timing — somehow buying at every bottom and selling at every peak — would produce only marginally better results than consistent monthly investing. The cost of waiting for the right time to invest is, on average, higher than the benefit of any timing advantage you might achieve.

The Target-Date Fund: The "Set It and Forget It" Option

If all of this feels like too many decisions, there's a single-fund solution: the target-date fund.

A target-date fund is a fund of funds — it holds a mix of stock index funds and bond index funds, automatically adjusting the allocation to become more conservative as your target retirement year approaches. You pick the fund closest to your retirement year (a "2035 fund" if you plan to retire around 2035), invest in it, and never think about asset allocation again.

Fidelity Freedom Index funds, Vanguard Target Retirement funds, and Schwab Target Date Index funds are all low-cost, well-designed options. Expense ratios typically run 0.10-0.15% for index-based versions.

The trade-off: target-date funds are slightly more expensive than holding the three funds yourself, and they don't let you customize your allocation. For many people — especially those who know they won't actively manage their portfolio — that trade-off is entirely worth it.

If your 401(k) offers a Vanguard or Fidelity target-date index fund and you're not sure what else to pick, that fund alone is a perfectly defensible choice.

Action Steps

Identify the index fund options in your 401(k). Look for funds with "index" in the name and check the expense ratios. If multiple index funds are available, find the ones tracking the S&P 500 or Total Market and prioritize those.

Calculate your target asset allocation. Use the 120-minus-age rule as a starting point (120 - your age = stock percentage). Adjust up or down based on your genuine risk tolerance and time horizon.

If you have an IRA or will be opening one, choose your brokerage and identify your three-fund portfolio holdings. For Fidelity: FZROX, FZILX, FXNAX (all zero or near-zero expense ratios). For Vanguard: VTI, VXUS, BND.

Set up automatic contributions to every account you're funding. Automation removes the willpower requirement. Schedule the transfer to happen on payday, before the money integrates into your spending.

Write down your investing rules in advance: "If the market drops 20%, I will not sell. I will continue my automatic contributions." Then don't look at your balance more than once per quarter. Frequent checking increases panic selling. Your job is not to manage the market — it's to stay invested in it.

Chapter 6: Catch-Up Contributions and Tax Advantages for People Over 50

Somewhere in the tax code, buried between rules that benefit corporations and provisions that help people with very specific circumstances, there is a collection of policies that were put there specifically for you — the person who didn't accumulate as much retirement savings as they "should" have and needs to move faster now.

Catch-up contributions are one of those policies. But they're just the beginning. The tax system contains multiple advantages that become more valuable as you get older, and most people over 50 aren't using all of them.

This chapter is about maximizing those advantages — not because you're playing catch-up (though you might be), but because you've earned access to a set of tools that weren't available to you at 30. Use them.

Catch-Up Contributions: The Basics

When the IRS sets annual contribution limits for retirement accounts, it also allows people 50 and older to contribute additional amounts — the "catch-up contribution." These aren't a special program you have to apply for. They're automatically available once you turn 50, and they're significant.

401(k), 403(b), and 457(b) plans (2025):

Standard limit: $23,500

Catch-up contribution (50+): $7,500

Total for those 50+: $31,000 per year

IRA (Traditional or Roth) (2025):

Standard limit: $7,000

Catch-up contribution (50+): $1,000

Total for those 50+: $8,000 per year

SIMPLE IRA (2025):

Standard limit: $16,500

Catch-up contribution (50+): $3,500

Total for those 50+: $20,000 per year

HSA (2025):

Standard limit: $4,300 individual / $8,550 family

Catch-up contribution (55+): $1,000

Note: HSA catch-up begins at 55, not 50

SEP-IRA and Solo 401(k): Catch-up contributions for Solo 401(k) follow the same 401(k) rules — $7,500 additional for those 50+. SEP-IRA has no catch-up contribution provision.

The total potential annual contribution for someone over 50 using a 401(k) and IRA: $31,000 + $8,000 = $39,000 per year. For the self-employed using a Solo 401(k) and IRA: potentially higher still, depending on income.

SECURE 2.0: The New Rules That Changed the Game

In 2022 and 2023, Congress passed two pieces of legislation collectively called SECURE 2.0 that significantly expanded retirement savings options. These changes are still being phased in, and many Americans — including some financial advisors — don't fully understand them yet. Here are the most important ones for late starters:

Higher catch-up contributions at 60-63: Starting in 2025, people between ages 60 and 63 get an even larger catch-up contribution for 401(k) and similar accounts. The limit is the greater of $10,000 or 150% of the standard 2024 catch-up amount, indexed for inflation. In practice, this means those aged 60-63 can contribute approximately $34,750 to a 401(k) in 2025 — more than $11,000 above the standard limit.

This enhanced catch-up for ages 60-63 is one of the most significant legislative gifts for late starters in recent history. If you're in this age window, maximizing this contribution is a priority. At $34,750 per year in pre-tax contributions, the tax savings alone at a 22% marginal rate amount to over $7,600 per year.

Roth catch-up requirement for high earners: Beginning in 2026, employees who earned more than $145,000 (adjusted for inflation) in the prior year must make catch-up contributions to a Roth 401(k) rather than a traditional pre-tax account. This affects planning for higher earners — worth discussing with a financial advisor if this applies to you.

Delayed required minimum distributions: The age at which you must start withdrawing from traditional retirement accounts (Required Minimum Distributions, or RMDs) has been pushed back. Under SECURE 2.0, the RMD starting age is now 73, increasing to 75 in 2033. This gives your investments more time to grow tax-deferred, and it gives you more flexibility in planning your retirement income.

Emergency savings provisions: SECURE 2.0 added a new ability to withdraw up to $1,000 per year from a retirement account for genuine emergencies without paying the 10% early withdrawal penalty. This reduces the psychological barrier of investing money that feels "locked up" — one of the most common reasons people avoid contributing to retirement accounts.

The Math on Maxing Out: What the Extra Contributions Actually Buy

Let's run through some concrete numbers to illustrate why these catch-up provisions matter so much.

Consider Diana, who is 52 and currently contributing $800 per month ($9,600 per year) to her 401(k). She has $42,000 in the account already. Her employer matches 50% up to 6% of salary. She earns $85,000.

Current scenario: At 7% average annual returns retiring at 67, Diana's 401(k) grows to approximately $640,000 (including employer match).

If Diana captures the full catch-up: She increases contributions to $31,000 per year (roughly $2,583 per month). This requires redirecting about $1,783 more per month from other spending — aggressive but achievable if she's committed. Retiring at 67, her account grows to approximately $1.1 million.

The difference: roughly $460,000 in retirement savings from aggressive use of catch-up provisions. That's not a rounding error.

Now consider Robert, who turns 61 in 2025 and has $180,000 in his 401(k). Under the new 60-63 enhanced catch-up, he can contribute up to $34,750 to his 401(k) this year. If he maximizes that for three years (ages 61, 62, and 63) while earning 7%, the additional contributions alone — above the standard limit — add approximately $35,000 to his portfolio compared to the standard catch-up. Combined with full contributions and employer match, his portfolio at 67 looks meaningfully different than it would have under the old rules.

Tax Bracket Management: A Tool Available Only to Those With Flexibility

One of the underappreciated advantages of being a deliberate late-start investor is that you can make strategic decisions about which accounts to fund based on your current and projected tax situation.

This is called tax bracket management — the practice of deliberately distributing income and contributions across years to minimize the total taxes paid over your lifetime.

The Roth conversion opportunity: Traditional IRA and 401(k) money will be taxed when you withdraw it in retirement. If you're currently in a lower tax bracket than you expect to be later — perhaps between jobs, in a lower-income year, or in the years between early retirement and when Social Security begins — you can convert traditional account money to a Roth IRA. You pay taxes on the converted amount at your current (lower) rate, and all future growth is tax-free.

The window between retirement (say, 60-65) and when Social Security begins (62-70) is often called the "Roth conversion window." Many retirees are in a surprisingly low tax bracket during this period because they haven't yet begun taking Social Security or RMDs. That lower bracket is an opportunity to convert pre-tax money to Roth at a lower tax cost.

For example: a couple who retires at 62 with $600,000 in traditional IRA assets and no Social Security or pension income until 67 might find themselves in the 12% federal tax bracket if their only income is a modest portfolio withdrawal. Converting $40,000-$60,000 per year to Roth during this window, paying 12% tax on the conversion, locks in that low rate before RMDs and Social Security push them into the 22% bracket later. The math on this can be compelling — potentially tens of thousands of dollars in lifetime tax savings.

Tax-loss harvesting: In taxable investment accounts, you can sell investments that have declined in value to realize a tax loss, which offsets capital gains elsewhere in your portfolio (or up to $3,000 of ordinary income per year). The money doesn't disappear — you reinvest it immediately in something similar. This is an advanced strategy, but worth knowing about as your taxable investment account grows.

Managing ordinary income in retirement: Having a mix of account types — Traditional 401(k)/IRA, Roth, and taxable accounts — gives you maximum flexibility in retirement to draw from different buckets in different years to control your taxable income. This is called tax diversification, and it's one of the strongest arguments for building Roth assets even when Traditional contributions might save slightly more tax now.

Required Minimum Distributions: Planning Ahead

A required minimum distribution (RMD) is the minimum amount the IRS requires you to withdraw from traditional retirement accounts each year, starting at age 73 (75 under current law if born after 1960). The IRS wants its tax money eventually, and RMDs are how they ensure that tax-deferred accounts don't grow indefinitely.

RMDs are calculated by dividing your account balance at the end of the prior year by a life expectancy factor from an IRS table. At 73, the factor is approximately 26.5, so a $500,000 account would require roughly $18,867 in withdrawals that year. At 80, the factor drops to about 20.2, meaning a $500,000 account would require $24,752 — a meaningfully larger required withdrawal.

The potential problem: if you have large traditional account balances and haven't done Roth conversions or other tax planning, your RMDs can push you into a higher tax bracket than expected — potentially making your Social Security partially taxable, increasing your Medicare premiums (through IRMAA surcharges), and creating a larger-than-anticipated tax bill.

Consider a retiree who has $1.2 million in a traditional IRA at age 73. Their RMD is approximately $45,000. Combined with Social Security of $28,000, their gross income is $73,000 — pushing them into the 22% tax bracket and potentially triggering IRMAA Medicare surcharges. If they had done Roth conversions in their early 60s when income was lower, that $1.2 million in traditional accounts might be $800,000 in traditional and $400,000 in Roth — reducing RMDs to roughly $30,000, and total taxable income to $58,000, staying in the 12% bracket.

Planning for RMDs is a reason to:

Consider Roth conversions during lower-income years before 73

Be strategic about which accounts you draw down first in early retirement

Run projections with a financial planner or tax advisor at least 10 years before you expect RMDs to begin

Roth accounts have no RMDs during the original owner's lifetime — another reason late starters might lean toward building Roth assets.

Working with a Financial Advisor: When It's Worth It

Most of this book is designed to help you do as much as possible yourself, because the evidence shows that low-cost index fund investing done consistently beats most professional management. But there are situations where a fee-only financial advisor adds genuine value for late starters:

Tax planning involving Roth conversions, RMD projections, and multi-year tax bracket management

Social Security claiming strategy optimization (more on this in Chapter 7)

Medicare and long-term care insurance decisions

Estate planning implications of retirement accounts

Complex situations involving a business, divorce, inheritance, or pension

The key distinction is "fee-only" — an advisor who charges you a flat fee or hourly rate, not one who earns commissions from selling you products. The National Association of Personal Financial Advisors (NAPFA) has a directory of fee-only advisors. A few hundred dollars spent on a one-time comprehensive retirement review can be worth significantly more in clarity and optimization.

Even a single consultation focused specifically on your Roth conversion strategy and Social Security claiming decision —

two areas with enormous potential impact for late starters — can pay for itself many times over in optimized lifetime outcomes.

The HSA Double-Down Strategy for Late Starters Over 55

If you're over 55 and eligible for an HSA (meaning you have a High Deductible Health Plan), the combination of HSA catch-up contribution and investment strategy deserves its own attention.

At 55+, you can contribute $9,550 per year for family coverage (the $8,550 family limit plus the $1,000 catch-up). Both contributions are tax-deductible. Unlike a traditional IRA or 401(k), HSA money used for qualified medical expenses is never taxed — not on the way in, not on the growth, not on the withdrawal.

The optimal approach for someone who can afford it: maximize HSA contributions, invest the entire balance in low-cost index funds, and pay all current medical expenses out of pocket from regular income. Every year you can do this, you're building a tax-free pool of money specifically for the healthcare expenses that will be substantial in retirement. Dental, vision, hearing aids, Medicare premiums, long-term care insurance premiums — all can be paid from an HSA tax-free.

At $9,550 per year invested in index funds for 10 years at 7% returns, the HSA balance alone would reach approximately $132,000. Every dollar of that can be withdrawn tax-free for medical expenses — effectively giving you $132,000 of healthcare spending that the government will never touch.

Action Steps

If you are 50 or older, verify that your 401(k) plan allows catch-up contributions and increase your contribution to capture them. Even adding an extra $200-$300 per month above your current amount starts closing the gap.

If you are between ages 60 and 63, research the enhanced catch-up limit that took effect in 2025 under SECURE 2.0. Your HR department or plan administrator can confirm the exact numbers for your plan.

Review your income this year and estimate your tax bracket. If you're in a lower-income year — perhaps part-year work, a transition between jobs, or an intentionally reduced schedule — consider whether a Roth IRA contribution or a Roth conversion makes sense at your current tax rate.

Request your annual Social Security statement at ssa.gov/myaccount, which also estimates your benefit at different claiming ages. Note the difference between claiming at 62, 67 (full retirement age for most), and 70. We'll use this in Chapter 7, but having the number now is valuable.

Calculate a simple projection: if you increased your monthly retirement contribution by $500 starting today and earned 7% annually until retirement, what would your additional balance be? Use a compound interest calculator (investor.gov has a free one). Seeing the actual number often creates the motivation that abstract urgency doesn't.

Timing Catch-Up Contributions for Maximum Impact

The mechanics of how you deploy catch-up contributions can matter as much as the amount. Here are the key timing considerations:

Front-load early in the year: If your financial situation allows, increasing contributions early in the calendar year — rather than in December — gives each contribution more time to grow. The difference between contributing in January versus December is 11 additional months of investment growth. On $7,500 in catch-up contributions at 7%, that timing difference adds roughly $435 in growth per year — modest, but it accumulates.

Coordinate with bonus income: Many workers receive annual bonuses in the first quarter. This is an ideal opportunity to temporarily increase your 401(k) contribution percentage to capture a larger portion of the bonus. Since bonuses are W-2 income, they're subject to 401(k) withholding at whatever rate you've set. Raising your contribution rate to 50% or 80% in the month you expect your bonus captures significantly more pre-tax money.

The Roth consideration in catch-up years: During your highest-earning years (typically 50s), Traditional pre-tax contributions save the most in current-year taxes. But those earnings go into accounts that will eventually require RMDs and generate taxable income in retirement. Each catch-up dollar directed to a Roth account instead avoids this future tax entirely. The optimal strategy for many late starters: use Traditional for the standard contribution limit, and use the catch-up portion for Roth — converting the highest-marginal-rate money into tax-free retirement income.

Using investment windfalls: An inheritance, business sale, or other windfall can be directed to a Roth IRA (up to the $8,000 annual limit for those 50+) or invested in a taxable brokerage account. Many late starters receive inheritances in their 50s or early 60s from aging parents — a difficult circumstance that sometimes provides a significant financial boost. Knowing in advance how you'd deploy such funds (rather than making impulsive decisions in an emotionally difficult time) is valuable.

Estate Planning and Account Beneficiaries: The Catch-Up You Can't Afford to Skip

Late starters focused on contribution rates and investment returns often neglect another form of financial planning that becomes increasingly urgent in your 50s and 60s: estate planning.

This isn't primarily about wealth — it's about control. Without proper estate planning, your retirement accounts and other assets may not flow to the people you intend, at the time you intend, in the way you intend.

Beneficiary designations: Every retirement account (401(k), IRA, Roth IRA) and life insurance policy has a beneficiary designation — a form you filled out (or didn't) when you opened the account. These designations override your will. A 401(k) that names your ex-spouse as beneficiary will go to your ex-spouse even if your will says otherwise. Review and update beneficiary designations on all accounts now. This takes 15 minutes and is one of the most impactful estate planning steps you can take.

Primary and contingent beneficiaries: Always name both. A primary beneficiary receives the account if they survive you. If they don't, the contingent beneficiary receives it. Without a contingent beneficiary, the account may go through probate — a slow, expensive, and public legal process.

Inherited IRA rules for beneficiaries: SECURE 2.0 changed the rules for inherited IRAs significantly. Most non-spouse beneficiaries who inherit a traditional IRA now must withdraw all funds within 10 years of the original owner's death (with some exceptions). This has tax planning implications — large inherited IRA balances forced into 10-year withdrawals can significantly increase a beneficiary's tax liability in those years. If you're building large traditional IRA balances and plan to leave them to children or other beneficiaries, this is a reason to consider Roth conversions that reduce the traditional balance.

Beyond accounts: A complete estate plan also includes a will, healthcare directive (specifying medical treatment preferences if you can't speak for yourself), durable power of attorney (authorizing someone to manage your financial affairs if incapacitated), and potentially a trust if your estate is complex. A consultation with an estate attorney is relatively affordable and can prevent enormously expensive consequences down the line.

Estate planning isn't morbid — it's an act of care for the people who matter to you. And for late starters who are building their wealth faster and later than planned, ensuring that wealth flows correctly when the time comes is part of the complete financial picture.

Chapter 7: Social Security — Understanding What You'll Get and How to Optimize It

Social Security is probably the most misunderstood component of American retirement planning. Some people dismiss it, assuming it won't exist by the time they retire. Others count on it as their primary income source, which it may not fully cover. A significant number make the default claiming decision — starting at 62 — without ever calculating what it costs them over their lifetime.

For late starters especially, Social Security deserves deep attention. Because here's the thing: you've been paying into it your entire working life. It is a real asset. Its value is determined by decisions you make in the years before you retire. And optimizing those decisions can be worth tens of thousands — sometimes more than $100,000 — over the course of your retirement.

Let's understand how it actually works.

How Your Benefit Is Calculated

Social Security retirement benefits are based on your lifetime earnings history. The Social Security Administration calculates your benefit using your highest 35 years of earnings, adjusted for inflation. If you worked fewer than 35 years, zeros are averaged in for the missing years — which can significantly reduce your benefit.

The calculation produces your Primary Insurance Amount (PIA) — the monthly benefit you'd receive if you claim at exactly your Full Retirement Age (FRA).

Full Retirement Age by birth year:

Born 1943-1954: FRA is 66

Born 1955: FRA is 66 and 2 months

Born 1956: FRA is 66 and 4 months

Born 1957: FRA is 66 and 6 months

Born 1958: FRA is 66 and 8 months

Born 1959: FRA is 66 and 10 months

Born 1960 or later: FRA is 67

The formula for calculating PIA is progressive — it replaces a higher percentage of income for lower earners and a lower percentage for higher earners. The average Social Security retirement benefit as of 2025 is approximately $1,930 per month, or about $23,000 per year. Maximum benefit (for those with high earnings claiming at FRA) is around $4,100 per month.

Your actual benefit estimate is available at ssa.gov/myaccount. Look at it now if you haven't. This is a real number that's been accumulating on your behalf for years.

The 35-year averaging rule has a particularly important implication for late starters who spent years in low-wage work, who took time away from the workforce for caregiving, or who had long gaps in employment. If you have fewer than 35 years of work history, working additional years (even part-time in retirement) directly replaces zero years in the calculation and can increase your benefit meaningfully. If your early work history includes very low-wage years, later high-earning years may push those early years out of the top-35 calculation, also increasing your benefit.

Early, On Time, or Late: The Claiming Decision

This is where Social Security planning becomes genuinely consequential.

You can begin claiming Social Security as early as age 62. Every month before your FRA that you claim, your benefit is permanently reduced. You can also delay claiming until as late as age 70, and every month you delay, your benefit permanently increases.

The numbers:

Claiming at 62: benefit is roughly 25-30% less than your FRA benefit (for those with FRA of 67)

Claiming at FRA (67): 100% of your PIA

Claiming at 68: approximately 108% of your PIA

Claiming at 69: approximately 116% of your PIA

Claiming at 70: approximately 124% of your PIA

That's not a small difference. If your FRA benefit is $2,200 per month, claiming at 62 gives you roughly $1,540. Waiting until 70 gives you roughly $2,728. The difference is nearly $1,200 per month — $14,400 per year — for the rest of your life, adjusted for inflation via cost-of-living adjustments.

The break-even calculation:

Claiming early gives you more checks but smaller ones. Claiming late gives you fewer but larger checks. The break-even point — where total lifetime benefits equalize — typically falls around age 80-82, depending on your specific benefit amounts.

If you live past the break-even point (which is roughly average life expectancy for a 65-year-old today), delaying increases your total lifetime benefit. If you die before the break-even point, you collected more by claiming early.

The practical implication: if you're in good health at 62-65 and have no pressing financial need to claim early, delaying until 70 is often — not always, but often — the financially optimal choice for a single individual.

However, the break-even analysis understates the value of delay for several reasons. Social Security benefits are adjusted annually for inflation (COLA adjustments), so a larger benefit grows more in absolute dollars over time. Social Security income is partially tax-free for lower-income retirees (and becomes less so at higher incomes) — a larger benefit may be taxed more, but the net-of-tax benefit is still larger. And if you're married, the higher earner's delayed benefit becomes the survivor benefit — more on this below.

Why Most People Claim Early (and Why That May Be a Mistake)

Approximately 30-40% of Americans claim Social Security at 62. This makes Social Security one of the most dramatic examples of people making significant financial decisions without fully understanding the consequences.

The reasons people claim early are often understandable:

They've left work and need income now

They're in poor health and worry they won't live to the break-even point

They don't trust that Social Security will continue to exist

They were told by someone that claiming early is smart because you get more checks

They simply didn't know the claiming rules in enough detail to make a deliberate choice

The problem is that for many people, especially those in reasonably good health with no immediate income need, claiming at 62 is one of the most expensive decisions of their retirement — they just don't know it at the time.

Consider a strategy called "bridge to 70": if you retire at 62 or 65 but can draw from savings, a pension, or part-time work to cover expenses, you can let Social Security grow until 70. Every year of delay from FRA to 70 increases your benefit by 8% — a guaranteed 8% return, which beats most investments on a risk-adjusted basis.

Contrast two people with a $2,200 FRA benefit and $200,000 in savings:

Person A claims at 62 ($1,540/month), preserves their savings by relying on Social Security.

Person B claims at 70 ($2,728/month), draws down $75,000 from savings between 67 and 70 as a bridge.

By 85, Person B has received significantly more in cumulative Social Security benefits and has had their savings deplete more slowly once Social Security started because the larger check covers more of their expenses. The $75,000 used as a bridge is often worth it.

Spousal Benefits: The Overlooked Multiplier

If you're married, Social Security becomes even more complex — and more valuable — because spouses are entitled to benefits based on each other's earnings records.

Spousal benefit basics:

A lower-earning spouse can claim up to 50% of the higher-earning spouse's FRA benefit

The higher-earning spouse must have filed for their own benefit for the spousal benefit to be available

Spousal benefits are also reduced for early claiming — claiming a spousal benefit at 62 gives you about 32-35% of the higher earner's benefit, not 50%

Spousal benefits do not increase by delaying past FRA — only your own benefit grows from delayed claiming

Survivor benefits: This is where spousal coordination becomes crucial. When one spouse dies, the surviving spouse keeps the higher of the two benefits and loses the lower one. If the higher earner claimed early at a reduced benefit, the surviving spouse inherits that reduced benefit — potentially for decades.

The most common strategy for married couples: the higher earner delays claiming as long as possible (ideally to 70) to maximize the survivor benefit, while the lower earner claims earlier to provide income in the meantime. This is not universal — health, age differences, and financial need all modify the optimal approach — but the survivor benefit consideration is the single most important factor many couples overlook.

Consider Carol and James, both 67 and entering retirement. Carol's FRA benefit is $2,400; James's is $1,100. If Carol claims immediately at her FRA, James can claim the spousal benefit of 50% of Carol's FRA benefit ($1,200) rather than his own $1,100, giving them $3,600/month combined. When Carol eventually dies, James keeps $2,400 (her benefit) for the rest of his life. Had Carol delayed to 70 ($2,976/month), the couple would have drawn only James's income for three years, but James's survivor benefit would be $2,976 instead of $2,400 — $576 more per month, every month, for the rest of his life. In 10 years of James's survival, that's $69,120 in extra income.

Will Social Security Still Exist When You Retire?

This question deserves a direct answer, because the anxiety around it drives many people to claim early unnecessarily.

The Social Security trust fund, which supplements payroll tax revenue to pay benefits, is projected by the Social Security

Administration's own actuaries to be depleted by around 2033-2035 if Congress takes no action. At that point, current payroll taxes alone would cover approximately 77-80% of scheduled benefits.

This is a funding challenge, not a program failure. It means:

Social Security is very unlikely to simply disappear

Benefits could be reduced if Congress doesn't act — but history suggests Congress will act (they've modified Social Security eight times since 1983, always preventing scheduled cuts)

The politically realistic scenarios include: benefit reductions for younger workers, increased payroll taxes, adjustments to full retirement age, means-testing at high income levels, or some combination

For people who are currently in their 40s or 50s, planning on receiving at least 75-80% of your projected benefit is a reasonable conservative assumption. Planning on zero is overly pessimistic and will cause you to make decisions (like claiming early "before it runs out") that are almost certainly not in your best interest.

Divorced and Widowed Individuals: Important Rules

Social Security has specific provisions for those who are divorced or widowed that can significantly affect planning.

Divorced individuals:

If you were married for at least 10 years and are currently unmarried, you can claim a spousal benefit based on your ex-spouse's earnings record

You don't need to coordinate with your ex — they don't need to know, and their benefits aren't affected

You can claim spousal benefits as early as 62 if your ex is also at least 62 (and has filed for benefits, or has been divorced for at least 2 years)

This doesn't prevent you from switching to your own benefit later if it becomes larger

Many divorced individuals don't know this benefit exists. If you were married for 10+ years and have a lower earnings record than your ex-spouse, this can meaningfully change your Social Security picture. Check with the SSA before assuming your benefit is based solely on your own work history.

Widowed individuals:

You can claim survivor benefits as early as age 60 (50 if disabled)

Survivor benefits are up to 100% of the deceased spouse's benefit (including any delayed claiming credits they accumulated)

One powerful strategy: claim reduced survivor benefits early to provide income while allowing your own retirement benefit to grow to age 70, then switch to your own benefit

If you're divorced or widowed, a consultation specifically about your Social Security claiming options — with a fee-only financial planner or through your local Social Security office — can be genuinely valuable.

Working While Receiving Social Security

Working while receiving Social Security before your FRA can temporarily reduce your benefits — but the money isn't lost; it's added back to your benefit once you reach FRA.

The earnings test (before FRA):

In 2025, if you're under FRA for the full year: $1 in benefits is withheld for every $2 you earn above $22,320

In the year you reach FRA: $1 withheld for every $3 earned above $59,520 (for the months before your FRA birthday)

After FRA: no earnings limit — you can earn any amount while receiving full benefits

This earnings test is one reason some people delay starting Social Security until they've fully retired or at least reduced their work significantly.

It also means that if you retire early, take Social Security at 62, and then find yourself back in part-time work earning $40,000 per year, your benefits will be substantially reduced. That reduction is recalculated and credited back at FRA, but you won't receive the withheld benefits as a lump sum — they're added to your monthly benefit going forward, requiring years to recover. Understanding this rule prevents some costly surprises.

Action Steps

Log into ssa.gov/myaccount and review your Social Security statement. Note your estimated benefit at 62, at your full retirement age, and at 70. These three numbers are the raw material for your claiming strategy.

Check your earnings history on the Social Security statement for accuracy. If you worked fewer than 35 years, identify whether additional working years before retirement could replace some low-earning or zero years and increase your benefit.

If you're married, calculate both spouses' projected benefits and run a basic break-even analysis. Resources like Open Social Security (opensocialsecurity.com) and the AARP Social Security Benefits Calculator provide free tools to compare different claiming strategies.

If you're divorced from a marriage that lasted 10+ years, check whether you may be eligible for spousal benefits based on your ex's earnings record. This is a benefit many divorced individuals don't claim because they don't know it exists.

Build Social Security income into your retirement projection in Chapter 11. Use 75-80% of your projected benefit as a conservative estimate if you're concerned about funding shortfalls. Include it in your monthly retirement income calculation alongside your investment withdrawals.

Cost-of-Living Adjustments: The Inflation Protection Built Into Social Security

One feature of Social Security that is consistently underappreciated in early retirement planning is the annual

Cost-of-Living Adjustment (COLA). Every year, Social Security benefits increase by a percentage tied to the Consumer Price Index for Urban Wage Earners and Clerical Workers (CPI-W).

This matters enormously for long-term retirement planning. In years with significant inflation — 2021-2023 saw COLAs of 5.9%, 8.7%, and 3.2% respectively — Social Security benefits grew significantly while inflation eroded the purchasing power of fixed income sources. A $2,000 monthly benefit in 2019 had grown to approximately $2,600 by 2024 through COLA adjustments alone.

The compounding impact of COLA over decades is substantial. A $2,400 monthly Social Security benefit that receives 2.5% COLA annually for 20 years grows to approximately $3,930 per month. A $1,540 early-claimed benefit receiving the same COLA grows to only $2,524. The gap between delayed and early claiming widens not just from the initial difference but from the fact that COLA is applied to a larger starting number each year.

This is one of the strongest arguments for delayed claiming: you're not just locking in a larger initial benefit — you're locking in a larger base for every future COLA adjustment, for the rest of your life.

Inflation and investment portfolio comparison: Your investment portfolio also needs to outpace inflation. If your portfolio earns 7% and inflation runs 3%, your real return is about 4%. Social Security, by contrast, is fully indexed to inflation by design. This makes Social Security one of the most inflation-protective income sources in retirement — a characteristic that becomes increasingly valuable as you age and your portfolio potentially becomes more conservative.

Social Security Taxation: How Your Benefits Are Taxed

Many people don't realize that Social Security benefits can be subject to federal income tax — up to 85% of your benefit can be included in your taxable income depending on your total income.

The calculation uses your "combined income" — adjusted gross income plus non-taxable interest plus half of your Social Security benefits.

Combined income below $25,000 (single) or $32,000 (married): no Social Security is taxed

Combined income between $25,000-$34,000 (single) or $32,000-$44,000 (married): up to 50% of benefits taxable

Combined income above $34,000 (single) or $44,000 (married): up to 85% of benefits taxable

This taxation threshold has not been adjusted for inflation since it was set in 1984, meaning more and more retirees pay taxes on their Social Security with each passing decade. A middle-income retiree with a $2,400/month Social Security benefit, a $25,000 IRA withdrawal, and $3,000 in investment income will likely have at least 50-85% of their Social Security benefit included in taxable income.

The practical implication: retirement tax planning should account for Social Security taxation. Drawing from Roth accounts (which don't count toward combined income) rather than traditional IRA accounts can reduce the portion of Social Security that's taxable — in some cases saving thousands of dollars per year in federal taxes.

State taxation of Social Security varies: as of 2025, approximately 13 states tax Social Security benefits to some degree. If you're considering relocation in retirement, the state tax treatment of Social Security is a factor worth researching.

Chapter 8: Housing, Equity, and the Real Estate Question

For many Americans, their home is their largest asset. It's sitting there on the net worth statement, often representing 40, 50, or even 60% of their total wealth. And yet most people never include it in their retirement plan in any concrete way — it's just there, a given, a backdrop. That's a mistake.

Housing is one of the most complex and emotionally loaded financial decisions late starters face. It touches identity, family, stability, and community, not just balance sheets. But the financial dimensions are real and significant, and they deserve clear-eyed analysis.

This chapter looks at the full picture: what your home equity is actually worth, how it fits into a retirement plan, and the different strategic paths you might take — from downsizing to reverse mortgages to renting rather than owning.

Home Equity: What It Is and How to Think About It

Home equity is the difference between your home's current market value and what you still owe on the mortgage. If your home is worth $380,000 and you owe $210,000, your equity is $170,000.

That equity is real wealth — but it's illiquid wealth. Unlike money in a brokerage account, you can't spend home equity directly. To access it, you need to do something: sell the home, borrow against it, or use specific financial products like a reverse mortgage. Each option has different implications.

The other thing to understand about home equity is that it's not an investment in the traditional sense. The historical appreciation of U.S. home values, adjusted for inflation, is roughly 1% per year over the long term — significantly less than the real stock market return of about 7%. What homeownership provides is not investment growth but a form of forced savings (you build equity as you pay down the mortgage), housing cost stability over time, a potential source of funds in retirement, and in many cases, an asset to pass to heirs.

This doesn't mean homeownership is a bad decision — for many people it's excellent. It means treating your home as the cornerstone of your retirement plan, rather than your investment portfolio, is potentially risky. The people who say "my house is my retirement plan" are making a bet that their equity will be accessible when they need it, at a value that supports their lifestyle, in a housing market that cooperates. Those conditions don't always hold.

Scenario 1: Downsizing

For many late starters, the most powerful housing strategy is downsizing — selling a larger home, buying or renting something smaller and less expensive, and deploying the freed equity into retirement accounts or investment accounts.

Here's how the math can look:

Sandra is 58, owns a four-bedroom home worth $450,000, with $140,000 remaining on the mortgage. Her equity is $310,000. Her children are grown and gone, and the house feels large and expensive to maintain — property taxes, utilities, insurance, and maintenance consume about $3,200 per month.

She downsizes to a two-bedroom condo worth $250,000, which she buys with cash from the sale proceeds. After transaction costs (roughly 6-8% on the sale, plus moving and buying costs), she nets approximately $200,000 after paying off the mortgage. She invests that $200,000 in a diversified portfolio.

The new condo has expenses of about $1,500 per month (HOA fees, property taxes, insurance). Monthly savings: approximately $1,700. She redirects that $1,700 per month into her retirement accounts.

Over 9 years to retirement at 67, the $200,000 invested at 7% grows to roughly $372,000, and the additional monthly contributions add another $255,000. Total from this one decision: over $600,000 in additional retirement assets.

This is a dramatic example, but the principle holds even at smaller scales. The family home after the children leave is often one of the single largest untapped financial resources for late starters.

Emotional reality: Downsizing is hard. The family home carries memories and meaning. Many people resist it even when the financial logic is clear. There's no objectively right answer — but going into the decision with clear numbers, rather than avoiding the question entirely, lets you make a genuine choice rather than a default one.

The timing of downsizing also matters. Real estate transaction costs — agent commissions, closing costs, moving expenses — typically run 7-10% of the home's value when you account for both sides of a transaction. On a $400,000 home, that's $28,000-$40,000 in friction. Downsizing makes sense earlier rather than later, because the freed equity has more time to work in an investment account.

Scenario 2: Staying in Place

Not everyone should downsize — or wants to. Some strong reasons to stay:

You're in a low-cost-of-living area where your housing costs are already reasonable

Significant equity but equally significant mortgage remaining means the sale proceeds wouldn't be as large as expected

You genuinely use the space, care for aging parents, or have family regularly staying

Moving costs and transaction costs (real estate agent commissions, closing costs, moving expenses) would consume a significant portion of the equity gain

Your home is in a location with strong appreciation potential that you want to hold for heirs

If you stay, the key is to be deliberate about it. Pay off the mortgage before retirement if possible — entering retirement without a mortgage payment significantly reduces your monthly income need. Make sure your housing costs as a percentage of retirement income are sustainable.

The traditional rule is to keep housing costs at or below 25-30% of gross income. In retirement, this becomes 25-30% of your retirement income — Social Security plus withdrawals plus any pension. Run the numbers and confirm your housing doesn't crowd out other essential expenses.

Staying in place also carries aging-in-place considerations. A four-bedroom colonial on three floors may be your dream home at 55 but present serious challenges at 80. If you plan to stay long-term, thinking ahead about potential modifications — first-floor bedroom capability, accessible bathrooms, no-step entries — can save significantly compared to crisis-mode modifications later, and can allow you to stay in a beloved home longer.

Scenario 3: Relocating to a Lower Cost of Living Area

One of the most powerful housing strategies for late starters isn't just downsizing in place — it's relocating to a significantly lower cost-of-living area while downsizing.

The math can be dramatic. A modest home in suburban Boston or Northern California might sell for $650,000-$900,000. A comparable or even superior home in the

Carolinas, Tennessee, portions of the Midwest, or the Mountain West might cost $250,000-$350,000. The equity release from this move — $300,000 to $600,000 or more — invested in a retirement portfolio can be transformative.

Beyond the housing purchase price, cost-of-living differences in property taxes, income taxes (some states have no income tax), groceries, and daily expenses can amount to $15,000-$30,000 per year in reduced spending — a reduction that compounds over decades of retirement.

The trade-offs are real: leaving community, proximity to family, medical facilities you've used for years. These are not trivial. But running the numbers on a relocation scenario — even as a thought experiment — often reveals options people hadn't considered.

Scenario 4: Renting in Retirement

The idea of renting in retirement feels uncomfortable to many homeowners — like stepping backward. But rental can be a financially sound and even preferable strategy in retirement, and it deserves consideration without the cultural baggage.

The advantages of renting in retirement:

Maximum flexibility — you can relocate for health reasons, family proximity, or lower cost of living without the transaction costs of selling

No maintenance expenses — a burst pipe, a roof replacement, an HVAC failure is the landlord's problem

Fully liquid — all the capital that would have been in your home is in your portfolio, generating returns

Simpler estate planning — no complex asset to manage or transfer

The primary risk: rental costs can increase, and you're exposed to rent inflation without the protection of a fixed mortgage payment. In high-demand markets, rental costs have risen dramatically over the past decade.

If you own a home outright (no mortgage) entering retirement, selling and renting may or may not make sense depending on your local rent vs. buy economics, your expected longevity, and your desire for flexibility. Run the numbers specific to your location — the decision is highly regional.

Home Equity Line of Credit (HELOC) as Emergency Reserve

A HELOC is a line of credit secured by your home's equity, typically at relatively low interest rates compared to personal loans or credit cards. Some retirees and near-retirees use an open (unused) HELOC as an emergency reserve — the equivalent of a backup emergency fund that doesn't require keeping large amounts of cash in low-return savings accounts.

This approach has merit but carries real risk: a HELOC can be frozen or reduced by the lender during economic downturns (as many homeowners discovered in 2008-2009), precisely when you might need it most. It is not a substitute for a cash emergency fund but can supplement one.

The other important caveat: borrowing against your home in retirement must be done with great care. Taking out a HELOC and spending the proceeds is effectively spending your home equity — equity that could otherwise support you later in life or be passed to heirs.

The Reverse Mortgage: What It Is and When It Makes Sense

A reverse mortgage is a loan available to homeowners age 62 and older that allows you to borrow against your home equity without making monthly payments. The interest accrues and the loan becomes due when you die, sell the home, or move out permanently.

The most common type is the FHA-insured Home Equity Conversion Mortgage (HECM), which comes with federal protections including the guarantee that you'll never owe more than the home's value (important if home prices decline).

Potential uses:

Supplement retirement income for someone with significant home equity but insufficient savings

Enable a "bridge to 70" Social Security delay strategy — use reverse mortgage proceeds to cover living expenses while letting Social Security grow

Fund large healthcare or home modification costs

Provide income security for a surviving spouse who might otherwise need to sell the home

Important limitations and costs:

High upfront costs: mortgage insurance premiums, origination fees, closing costs can total $15,000-$25,000 or more

The loan grows over time, consuming equity that might otherwise go to heirs

The home must remain your primary residence — if you need to move to assisted living, the loan becomes due

Non-borrowing spouses have protections under current rules but the situation is complex

Reverse mortgages have a troubled history — there were widespread abuses in earlier decades — but the current HECM product with its federal insurance and mandatory counseling requirement is a legitimate tool. It's not right for everyone, but for a homeowner with substantial equity and a retirement income gap, it deserves serious consideration.

The "standby" HECM strategy: some financial planners recommend opening a reverse mortgage line of credit early in retirement — before you need it — and letting it grow (HECM credit lines grow over time based on interest rates and the age of the borrower). This line of credit is then available as a liquidity reserve during market downturns, allowing you to avoid selling investments at depressed prices and instead draw from the HECM temporarily.

Real Estate as Investment (Beyond Your Home)

Some late starters ask whether buying rental property could help close the retirement gap. The answer is: it's possible, but it's often not the right tool for people starting this process in their 40s or 50s.

Rental real estate is an active business, not a passive investment. It requires finding and vetting tenants, handling maintenance and repairs, navigating legal requirements, and managing vacancies. The return can be good, but so can the headaches.

If you're considering rental property, a few honest questions:

Do you have enough capital for a meaningful down payment (typically 20-25% for investment property) without depleting emergency funds or retirement accounts?

Can you handle the property management demands while still working full-time?

Have you stress-tested the numbers with realistic vacancy rates, maintenance costs, and property management fees?

Is this actually a better return than simply investing the down payment in index funds?

Real estate investment trusts (REITs) — specifically REIT index funds — offer exposure to real estate returns without the operational headaches. A diversified REIT index fund within your portfolio may be a more practical approach to real estate exposure for most late starters.

Action Steps

Add your home to your net worth statement with a current estimated market value (check Zillow, Redfin, or Realtor.com for comparable sales). This gives you an accurate picture of your total wealth, not just your financial account balances.

Calculate your monthly housing cost: mortgage/rent, property taxes, insurance, utilities, and maintenance (estimate 1-2% of home value annually for maintenance). Compare this to your monthly income. If housing is above 35% of take-home pay, this is a financial strain worth addressing.

If you own a home larger than you currently need, run the downsizing math for your specific situation. What would you net after transaction costs and paying off the mortgage? What would you spend on a smaller home? What would the monthly savings be? Don't make a decision — just see the numbers.

If you have significant home equity and are approaching retirement without sufficient savings, research whether a HELOC or reverse mortgage consultation makes sense for your situation. The National Reverse Mortgage Lenders Association (nrmla.org) has a consumer resources section with unbiased information.

Look up the rent-vs-buy ratio in your area (annual rental costs divided by home purchase price). In markets where this ratio is above 20-25x, renting is often financially competitive with owning. In markets below 15-18x, owning tends to be more advantageous. This ratio helps ground the rent vs buy decision in local market reality.

Property Tax Strategies for Retirement Planning

Property taxes are a fixed housing expense that many homeowners pay on autopilot without examining potential relief options. In retirement, when income is fixed and every dollar counts, this is worth attention.

Homestead exemptions: Most states offer some form of property tax reduction for primary residences. These exemptions vary widely — some are modest ($1,000-$5,000 off assessed value), others are substantial. Florida, for example, offers a $50,000 homestead exemption.

Senior property tax exemptions: Many states and counties offer additional property tax reductions specifically for residents over a certain age (commonly 65) or below certain income thresholds. Some programs freeze property values for assessment purposes, protecting retirees from rising assessments even as property values increase. Texas's senior freeze, for example, locks the school district property tax component for homeowners over 65.

Circuit breaker programs: Named by analogy to electrical circuit breakers, these programs limit property taxes to a percentage of income for qualifying low-to-moderate-income homeowners. If your property taxes exceed a set percentage of your income, the excess may be refunded or credited.

These programs are administered locally and vary enormously. Contact your county tax assessor's office to understand what's available where you live. For a late-start retiree with a paid-off home and modest income, property tax relief programs can reduce annual housing expenses by $1,000-$5,000 — a meaningful annual improvement.

The Psychological Dimensions of Homeownership in Retirement Planning

The financial case for housing decisions rarely exists in a vacuum. For most people, the home isn't just an asset — it's identity, stability, and the place where the most important moments of life happened.

This matters for financial planning because it means decisions will be made with the heart as much as the spreadsheet, and that's not inherently wrong. The goal isn't to strip the emotion out of housing decisions — it's to make them with honest financial information alongside the personal considerations.

Some common psychological traps to watch for:

The "one day the kids will want this house" assumption. Many parents hold onto a large family home assuming their adult children will eventually want it. Adult children frequently don't — they have their own lives in different cities, different preferences in home styles, and often aren't in a position to take on the carrying costs. Have the actual conversation before assuming.

Status anchoring. Your home reflects your professional success and social standing in ways that feel real even when they're not financially rational. Downsizing can feel like admitting defeat — even when it would dramatically improve your financial situation. Naming this tendency helps you separate it from the decision.

Anchoring to purchase price. The price you paid for your home is financially irrelevant to the decision you're making today about whether to sell it. What matters is its current value and its future cost to maintain. People who bought at $180,000 and could now sell for $450,000 sometimes feel reluctant to sell because "we only paid $180,000" — but that's not actually relevant to the current decision.

Making housing decisions clearly — with numbers, with the emotional considerations honestly named and acknowledged

— leads to better outcomes than either ignoring the numbers or ignoring the human dimensions.

Chapter 9: Healthcare, Long-Term Care, and the Costs Nobody Plans For

If you've done the work of the previous chapters — mapped your finances, started investing, looked at your housing situation — there's one category that can undo all of it if you don't plan for it: healthcare.

Fidelity's annual retiree healthcare cost estimate for 2025 puts the number for a 65-year-old couple at roughly $315,000 over the course of retirement. That's not long-term care. That's not nursing home costs. That's Medicare premiums, supplemental insurance, copays, prescription drugs, dental, vision, and hearing — the routine healthcare expenses of two reasonably healthy people living into their 80s.

When that number appears in retirement planning conversations, it tends to produce one of two reactions: disbelief or paralysis. Neither helps. What helps is understanding where those costs come from and building them into your plan with the same rigor you bring to everything else.

Healthcare Before Medicare: The 65-Minus-Your-Retirement-Age Problem

Medicare begins at 65. If you retire before 65 — or even if you retire at 65 exactly — there's a coverage gap that requires planning.

If you retire early (before 65): You will need to find your own health insurance, and it will not be cheap.

Your options:

COBRA continuation: Keep your employer's plan for up to 18 months after leaving your job. The coverage is identical to what you had, but you now pay the full premium that your employer was subsidizing — often $700-$1,500 per month for an individual, $1,500-$2,500 for a family. Useful as a bridge but expensive.

ACA Marketplace plans: Available through healthcare.gov. Premiums are based on your income in retirement, and here's something many people miss: if your income (from investment withdrawals, Social Security, part-time work) is between 100% and 400% of the federal poverty level, you qualify for significant premium subsidies. In 2025, a couple at $50,000 income might pay dramatically less than face-rate premiums. The ACA calculator at healthcare.gov gives precise estimates.

Medicaid: If your income is below roughly 138% of the federal poverty level and you're in a Medicaid expansion state, you may qualify for Medicaid — essentially free or very-low-cost coverage. This is relevant for people in lower-income retirement situations or those in gap years between leaving work and claiming Social Security.

Spouse's employer plan: If your spouse is still working, staying on their employer plan is often the best option.

The strategic implication: if you plan to retire before 65, healthcare costs need to be explicitly budgeted, and keeping retirement income low enough to qualify for ACA subsidies may be a deliberate strategy worth considering in your withdrawal planning.

A crucial point that many people miss: Roth IRA withdrawals do not count as income for ACA subsidy calculations. If you have a Roth IRA and draw from it in your pre-Medicare years, those withdrawals are invisible to the ACA income calculation — allowing you to live on Roth distributions while maintaining low enough "income" to qualify for substantial premium subsidies. This can save thousands of dollars per year and is a compelling argument for building Roth assets while you're still working.

Medicare: What It Is and What It Doesn't Cover

Medicare is not free, and it doesn't cover everything. Understanding the structure is essential for accurate retirement planning.

Part A (Hospital Insurance):

Covers inpatient hospital stays, skilled nursing facility care (limited), hospice, and some home health

Free for most people (those who worked 40+ quarters and paid Medicare taxes)

Significant cost sharing: deductibles and copays apply, with no out-of-pocket maximum

Part B (Medical Insurance):

Covers doctor visits, outpatient care, preventive services, and durable medical equipment

Premium in 2025: $185 per month for those at standard income levels (higher for those above income thresholds — see IRMAA below)

20% coinsurance after deductible — no out-of-pocket cap

Part D (Prescription Drug Coverage):

Separate prescription drug plan, either standalone or through Medicare Advantage

Premiums vary by plan; average around $55-$85 per month in 2025

As of 2025, the Inflation Reduction Act caps annual out-of-pocket drug costs at $2,000 for Part D beneficiaries

Medicare Advantage (Part C):

Private insurance plans that bundle Part A, B, and usually D

Often include dental, vision, and hearing (which traditional Medicare does not cover)

May have lower premiums than original Medicare + Medigap but come with provider networks and prior authorization requirements

Can be a good option depending on your health needs and local plan offerings

Medigap (Medicare Supplement Insurance):

Private insurance that wraps around original Medicare to fill cost-sharing gaps

Eliminates or reduces the 20% coinsurance and deductible exposure

Premium varies significantly by plan type and age; commonly $150-$350 per month

Standardized plan letters (Plan G, Plan N, etc.) mean the coverage is identical across insurers — shop by price

The coverage gaps that Medicare doesn't cover, even with Medigap: dental care, vision exams and glasses, hearing aids, and most long-term care. These gaps require either out-of-pocket spending, supplemental coverage, or specific long-term care planning.

Enrollment timing matters enormously. Medicare enrollment outside of your Initial Enrollment Period (the 7-month window around your 65th birthday) triggers permanent premium penalties: 10% per year for Part B (no expiration), and 1% per month for Part D. Missing your IEP by even a year costs you

10% more per month on Part B premiums for the rest of your life. Set a reminder well in advance.

IRMAA: The Medicare Surcharge High Earners Don't See Coming

IRMAA stands for Income-Related Monthly Adjustment Amount — a Medicare surcharge for higher-income beneficiaries. If your Modified Adjusted Gross Income (MAGI) exceeds certain thresholds, your Medicare Part B and Part D premiums increase significantly.

2025 IRMAA thresholds (based on 2023 income):

Individual MAGI below $106,000 / Couple below $212,000: standard premium ($185/month Part B)

Individual $106,000-$133,000 / Couple $212,000-$266,000: $259/month

Individual $133,000-$167,000 / Couple $266,000-$334,000: $370/month

Individual $167,000-$200,000 / Couple $334,000-$400,000: $480/month

Higher income levels: up to $628/month per person

For someone taking large required minimum distributions from traditional retirement accounts, or doing substantial Roth conversions, or receiving Social Security plus significant investment income — IRMAA can add thousands of dollars per year to Medicare costs without warning.

This is one of the most compelling arguments for deliberate retirement income planning: understanding and managing your MAGI in retirement to minimize IRMAA exposure. Having a mix of Roth and traditional accounts gives you flexibility to control taxable income each year.

IRMAA uses a two-year lookback — your 2025 Medicare premiums are based on your 2023 income. This means a high-income year (from a Roth conversion, a large capital gain, or a lump-sum pension payment) can affect Medicare premiums two years later. Plan for this if you're undertaking large financial transactions.

Long-Term Care: The Expense That Can Eclipse Everything

Long-term care — the ongoing assistance with daily activities that becomes necessary when health declines to a certain point — is the single largest unplanned financial risk most retirees face.

The statistics are sobering:

About 70% of people who reach age 65 will need some form of long-term care during their lifetime

The average duration of long-term care need is approximately 3 years

Median annual cost of a private room in a nursing home: approximately $108,000 in 2025

Median annual cost of assisted living: approximately $64,000 in 2025

Median annual cost of full-time in-home care: approximately $75,000-$85,000 in 2025

A three-year nursing home stay at median cost would consume approximately $324,000. A five-year stay — not uncommon for conditions like Alzheimer's disease — approaches $540,000. These numbers can devastate retirement savings that took decades to build.

What Medicare covers: Medicare covers short-term skilled nursing facility care after a qualifying hospital stay — 100 days maximum, and with significant cost sharing after day 20. It does not cover custodial care (help with bathing, dressing, eating) that is not related to a medical condition being treated. Medicare is not a long-term care solution.

What Medicaid covers: Medicaid is the safety net program that covers long-term care for those who have spent down their assets to very low levels (typically $2,000-$8,000 in countable assets for an individual). "Spending down" to Medicaid qualification is a real planning strategy for some, but it means depleting almost everything you've accumulated. Medicaid planning is complex and state-specific — involving specific rules about asset transfers, exempt assets (your home, one car, certain prepaid expenses) — and requires a specialized elder law attorney.

Long-Term Care Insurance: The Declining Market and Its Alternatives

Traditional long-term care insurance was once straightforward — you paid premiums for coverage that would pay a daily benefit if you needed care. But the industry has struggled:

insurance companies underestimated how much care policyholders would actually use, leading to dramatic premium increases and many carriers exiting the market.

The current landscape:

Traditional standalone LTC policies are still available but significantly more expensive than they were 20 years ago

The ideal age to purchase traditional LTC insurance is roughly 55-65 — young enough to still qualify medically and lock in lower premiums, old enough that premiums remain manageable

Premium increases after purchase, while not guaranteed, have been common — budgeting for possible increases is prudent

Hybrid life insurance/LTC products: These combine a life insurance death benefit with a long-term care rider. You make a single premium or series of premiums; if you need long-term care, the death benefit is accessed for that purpose; if you don't, the full death benefit passes to heirs. These eliminate the "use it or lose it" problem of traditional LTC insurance. They tend to be expensive but offer more certainty.

Self-insuring: For those with substantial assets, self-funding long-term care — essentially accepting the risk and keeping earmarked funds in case they're needed — is a legitimate strategy. Generally this requires net worth of $2 million or more to absorb a worst-case long-term care event without threatening the remaining portfolio.

The middle path for most late starters: A combination of modest LTC coverage (shorter benefit period, lower daily benefit) combined with some self-insurance is often most practical. A policy that pays $150-$200 per day for three years doesn't cover everything, but it significantly reduces the financial damage of a care event.

Practical Planning for Healthcare Costs

Here's how to build healthcare costs into your retirement plan:

Pre-Medicare years (if you retire before 65): Budget $600-$1,200 per month for individual health insurance premiums (depending on income and ACA subsidy eligibility), plus out-of-pocket costs. Run your specific scenario through healthcare.gov's calculator.

Medicare years: Budget a baseline of $500-$700 per month per person for Part B premium, Part D, and Medigap or Medicare Advantage premiums combined. Add $2,000-$4,000 per year for out-of-pocket spending on copays, dental, vision, and hearing.

Long-term care contingency: Depending on your strategy, this might be an LTC insurance premium ($2,000-$5,000 per year), a self-insurance reserve, or a specific account earmarked for potential care expenses.

HSA utilization: If you've built an HSA (see Chapter 4), use it to fund dental, vision, hearing, and significant out-of-pocket medical costs tax-free. A well-funded HSA is one of the most valuable healthcare planning assets you can hold into retirement.

The mistake most late starters make with healthcare is treating it as a single line item rather than a complex, evolving cost category. Your healthcare expenses at 65 will look different from your expenses at 75, which will look different from your expenses at 85. Planning for the earlier decades without accounting for the later ones systematically underestimates total healthcare costs by a wide margin.

Action Steps

Estimate your healthcare costs between now and Medicare eligibility at 65 if you plan to retire before that age. Use healthcare.gov's calculator to estimate your ACA premium based on your projected retirement income.

Calculate your projected Medicare costs starting at 65. Use the baseline of $600-$700 per month per person for Part B, Part D, and supplemental coverage, and adjust based on your health history and expected utilization.

Research long-term care insurance options by getting quotes from two or three insurers. Focus on policies with a three-year benefit period, 90-day elimination period, and inflation protection. Compare these to the cost of self-insuring. The American Association for Long-Term Care Insurance (aaltci.org) has a directory of independent brokers.

If you have an HSA, maximize contributions immediately if eligible, and invest the balance in index funds rather than leaving it in the default money market account. Set up a system to track medical receipts going forward for potential future reimbursement.

Factor total annual healthcare costs into your retirement income projection in Chapter 11. A common planning figure is $12,000-$15,000 per year per person for healthcare in retirement at Medicare age, rising over time. Use this as a baseline unless your personal situation suggests significantly different numbers.

Managing Dental, Vision, and Hearing Costs: The Gaps That Add Up

The three most common out-of-pocket healthcare expenses that Medicare doesn't cover – dental, vision, and hearing – deserve their own planning section, because they're simultaneously significant and frequently overlooked.

Dental: Traditional Medicare provides almost no dental coverage. A single dental implant costs $3,000-$5,000; full mouth restoration for someone who deferred dental care can run $20,000-$50,000. Many retirees are shocked to face these costs after decades of employer-provided dental coverage.

Options: Medicare Advantage plans often include some dental coverage – this is one of the legitimate advantages of MA plans over original Medicare for people with dental needs. Standalone dental insurance for seniors is available but typically caps benefits at $1,000-$1,500 per year – barely enough for one crown. Dental schools provide quality care at significantly reduced rates, often 50-70% below market price. And some retirees find it cost-effective to travel to Mexico, Canada, or Central America for major dental procedures at a fraction of U.S. costs (dental tourism is a real and growing option for complex procedures).

Vision: Medicare covers eye exams related to medical conditions (glaucoma screening, diabetic eye disease) but not routine vision exams or corrective lenses. For the majority of retirees who need reading glasses or progressive lenses, vision costs of $300-$600 per year are typical. Medicare Advantage plans often include vision benefits. An HSA can be used for prescription eyewear.

Hearing: Hearing loss affects approximately one-third of people over 65 and two-thirds over 75. Hearing aids, which Medicare has historically not covered, cost $2,000-$7,000 per pair and typically need replacement every 5-7 years. The recent over-the-counter hearing aid regulations have significantly reduced prices for mild-to-moderate hearing loss — devices now available for $200-$1,500 may be adequate for many people. For those needing prescription hearing aids, some Medicare Advantage plans offer partial coverage.

Planning for dental, vision, and hearing costs requires either setting aside $500-$1,500 annually in a dedicated fund, choosing a Medicare Advantage plan with meaningful ancillary benefits, or utilizing HSA funds strategically.

The Caregiver Cost: When You're on Both Sides of Healthcare

For many late starters in their 50s and 60s, healthcare costs aren't just a personal planning issue — they're also a potential caregiving cost. The "sandwich generation" phenomenon — simultaneously caring for aging parents while still raising or supporting children — creates healthcare financial pressures from both directions.

Caring for an aging parent has direct costs: contributions to their care, medical copays you might cover on their behalf, modifications to your home if they move in, or out-of-pocket assisted living or home care costs. But the indirect costs are often larger: time away from work, career disruptions, stress-related health impacts on the caregiver.

Research consistently shows that informal (unpaid) caregiving costs caregivers an average of $303,000 in lost wages, benefits, and Social Security wealth over a lifetime. Late starters who spend years providing informal care for parents are often the same people who arrive at 55 with gaps in their own retirement savings — not because of irresponsibility, but because caregiving extracted a real financial cost.

If you anticipate caring for aging parents in the coming years, building this into your financial plan — not as a vague acknowledgment but as a budget line — matters. Depending on the level of care needed, you might budget $5,000-$20,000 per year in direct costs, plus a contingency fund for unexpected care needs.

And critically: having those conversations with your parents about their own financial and healthcare plans — what insurance they have, what their care preferences are, where their documents are — is one of the most important financial conversations a late starter can have. The alternative is crisis-mode decision-making under emotional duress, which is both worse for your parents and more expensive.

Chapter 10: Working Longer as a Strategy — The Math, the Options, and the Trade-offs

Let's talk about something that personal finance books often treat as a last resort, a consolation prize for people who didn't save enough: working longer.

It isn't either of those things. For late starters especially, working longer — even a few extra years — is one of the most powerful financial levers available, and the math behind it is dramatic. Whether you extend a traditional career, shift into consulting, take on part-time work, or redesign your work life to be sustainable for decades longer, the financial impact can be transformative.

This chapter isn't about telling you that you have to work until you drop. It's about making the decision deliberately — understanding exactly what additional working years buy you — so that you can choose the retirement timeline that actually fits your life.

The Math: Why Additional Working Years Are So Powerful

Working an extra year has three simultaneous effects on your retirement security, and the combination is more powerful than most people intuit:

Effect 1: You contribute more to your portfolio.

Every additional year of work is typically a year of maximum earning power and maximum savings capacity. If you're saving $2,000 per month and working an additional two years instead of retiring, that's $48,000 in new contributions before investment growth.

Effect 2: Your portfolio grows while untouched.

Every year you delay drawing down your investments is a year of growth. A $400,000 portfolio at 7% annual return grows to $428,000 in one year without a single contribution. At $500,000, that's a $35,000 gain in twelve months. The portfolio is at its largest when returns are most impactful.

Effect 3: You shorten the distribution period.

This is the effect people forget most often. If your portfolio needs to support 30 years of retirement versus 25 years, you can withdraw significantly less each year while maintaining the same probability of not running out of money. The standard "safe withdrawal rate" (the percentage you can withdraw annually without depleting your portfolio) increases meaningfully with shorter time horizons.

Let's put concrete numbers on this. Consider Raymond, age 59, with $280,000 in retirement savings. He's considering retiring at 62 versus 65.

If he retires at 62 and contributes $1,500 per month until then, his portfolio at retirement is approximately $390,000. That needs to last 25+ years.

If he retires at 65 and contributes $1,500 per month until then, his portfolio is approximately $600,000 — growing for three additional years while he continues contributing. Additionally, his portfolio only needs to last 22 years. Using the 4% safe withdrawal rate, $600,000 supports $24,000 per year from investments — versus $390,000 supporting about $15,600.

The three extra years bought him nearly $700 per month in sustainable retirement income. Plus, if he delays Social Security from 62 to 65, his benefit also increases (and if he waits to 67 or 70, even more so). The combined effect is substantial.

Effect 4: Social Security grows.

Each year you delay claiming Social Security between FRA and 70 adds 8% to your benefit — permanently, for life, inflation-adjusted. Working longer naturally facilitates Social Security delay, which can add hundreds of dollars per month to lifetime income.

The Safe Withdrawal Rate and Time Horizon

The "4% rule" was developed by financial planner Bill Bengen in 1994 based on historical market data. It holds that you can withdraw 4% of your portfolio in your first year of retirement, adjust that amount annually for inflation, and have a very high probability of your money lasting 30 years.

For late starters planning a shorter or longer retirement than 30 years, adjustments are needed:

| Retirement Duration | Conservative Withdrawal Rate |

40 years	3.2-3.5%
30 years	4.0%
25 years	4.5%
20 years	5.0-5.5%
15 years	6-7%

Working longer shortens your distribution period and therefore increases your safe withdrawal rate — another mathematical argument for the value of additional years.

These rates assume a diversified portfolio with a significant stock allocation. If you hold very conservative investments (mostly bonds), expected returns are lower and safe withdrawal rates decrease accordingly.

To make the table concrete: someone retiring with $400,000 at 62 (expecting a 30-year retirement) can safely withdraw about $16,000 per year. The same person retiring at 67 (expecting a 25-year retirement) can safely withdraw about $18,000 per year from the same $400,000. But in practice, five additional years of contributions and growth at 7% would likely grow that $400,000 to $600,000 or more — changing the sustainable withdrawal from $16,000 to approximately $27,000 per year. Every element compounds in the same direction.

Phased Retirement: Not a Binary Choice

Most people think of retirement as a switch — you're working, and then you're retired. But increasingly, the most financially and personally satisfying path is a phased transition.

Reduce hours at your current employer. Many organizations will allow employees approaching retirement age to shift to part-time, project-based, or consulting arrangements. The income reduction is significant but so is the lifestyle improvement — and the financial impact of even part-time income is substantial. Someone earning $30,000 per year part-time while drawing minimally from retirement accounts gives those accounts years of additional growth.

Teresa, a 62-year-old HR director, negotiated a four-day week with her employer rather than retiring outright. Her income dropped 20%, but she eliminated her commute, reduced childcare costs for a grandchild she was occasionally watching, and had time for the hobbies she'd been deferring. She continued full 401(k) contributions (catch-up eligible at 60+) for three years before full retirement. Her portfolio grew from $320,000 to $480,000 during those three years — a transformation she couldn't have achieved through full retirement at 62.

Bridge careers. Some late starters deliberately plan a "bridge career" — moving from their primary career into lower-stress, lower-demand work that they can sustain for additional years. A former marketing executive becomes a part-time marketing consultant. A nurse becomes a medical office administrator. A teacher becomes a tutor. The new role typically earns less but requires significantly less physical and emotional output.

Consulting or freelancing. For those with specialized skills, the transition to consulting can actually increase income in the near term (consultants typically charge hourly rates that significantly exceed their salaried equivalent) while offering maximum schedule flexibility. The trade-off: no employer benefits, which makes healthcare and retirement account management more self-directed – but the Solo 401(k) and SEP-IRA options discussed in Chapter 4 were designed for exactly this situation.

Encore careers. Some people spend their primary career in high-demand, high-compensation fields, then "retire" into second careers that are lower-paying but intrinsically more rewarding – nonprofit work, teaching, coaching, trades. These aren't financial strategies primarily; they're life design choices. But if income from an encore career even partially covers living expenses, the impact on portfolio longevity is significant.

Healthcare: The Hidden Cost of Early Retirement

We covered healthcare costs in Chapter 9, but it's worth connecting that material explicitly to the retirement timing question.

If your employer provides health insurance, early retirement before Medicare eligibility at 65 requires you to replace that coverage. For a 60-year-old couple with no ACA subsidies (because their income from investment withdrawals and Social Security exceeds ACA thresholds), private health insurance can easily cost $1,500-$2,500 per month – $18,000-$30,000 per year.

That's not a small number. For someone retiring at 62 and reaching Medicare at 65, three years of bridge health insurance can cost $54,000-$90,000 in premiums alone, not counting copays and out-of-pocket expenses.

Working until 65 eliminates this cost entirely for many people. If you have employer-sponsored insurance that you'd lose at retirement, extending your working years until 65 has significant financial value beyond the portfolio contributions and growth — you're also avoiding a major insurance expense.

This healthcare calculation changes the math dramatically for many people. A $1,800/month employer health insurance benefit (what you'd otherwise pay) is equivalent to a $21,600/year raise in real economic terms. For someone thinking "should I retire at 63 or 65?", the healthcare cost of those two extra years often totals $40,000-$50,000 — a non-trivial addition to the retirement ledger.

The Emotional and Health Dimensions

A chapter on working longer would be incomplete without acknowledging that this isn't purely a financial question.

The health argument for work: Research consistently shows that meaningful work contributes to cognitive health, social connection, purpose, and physical health — all factors associated with longer lifespan and better quality of life. The transition from full-time work to full-time leisure, without other purposeful activities to replace the structure, can be jarring and sometimes harmful.

The research on retirement timing and health is nuanced: early retirement from high-stress, physically demanding, or personally unfulfilling work tends to improve health outcomes. Retirement from engaging, socially connected, purposeful work can have more mixed results. The type of work matters enormously in this calculation.

The physical limits argument: Some jobs cannot be extended gracefully. Physically demanding work — construction, nursing, skilled trades, many service jobs — takes a real toll. Workers in these fields often have legitimate reasons to retire earlier, and building a plan that accounts for that reality is more important than forcing a generic "work until 67" framework onto a situation that doesn't fit.

The caregiver reality: Many people retire earlier than planned not because they chose to, but because they need to care for an aging parent, a sick spouse, or a grandchild. These are not financial failures — they're human realities. If caregiving has altered your retirement timeline, the planning focus shifts to making the most of the situation as it is, not the situation as you intended it to be.

When Early Retirement Is the Right Call

Not everyone should work longer, and there are situations where early retirement makes genuine sense:

Your health is significantly compromised and your ability to work is declining

You've reached adequate financial security and the additional years provide diminishing lifestyle returns relative to the freedom of retirement

Your job is causing significant stress, health damage, or misery that outweighs the financial benefit

You have a specific meaningful plan for retirement — significant projects, caregiving, travel, community involvement — that doesn't require continued work

Your partner's situation requires you to retire together at a specific time

The decision isn't whether working longer is "always better." It's whether, in your specific situation, the additional years of work are worth what you'd gain financially relative to what you'd give up in time, health, and lifestyle.

Part-Time Work in Retirement as a Safety Valve

Even after full retirement, part-time or project-based work can serve as a powerful financial safety valve — particularly in the early years of retirement when markets might be volatile.

The "sequence of returns" problem is one of the most dangerous aspects of early retirement: if markets decline significantly in the first few years of retirement while you're drawing down your portfolio, the damage to long-term wealth is disproportionately severe. Earning even $15,000-$20,000 per year from part-time work in the first three to five years of retirement dramatically reduces the required withdrawal rate and protects the portfolio during those vulnerable early years.

Consider two retirees, both with $500,000 portfolios at age 62, both needing $40,000 per year from their portfolio. One experiences a 30% market decline in year two of retirement. The other also experiences the same decline, but has $18,000 in part-time income, reducing portfolio withdrawals to $22,000 that year.

Five years later, the portfolio of the first retiree has been significantly damaged by the combination of large withdrawals during depressed prices. The second retiree's portfolio has largely recovered because withdrawals during the downturn were small. The $18,000 in part-time income during a bad market year was worth far more than $18,000 in pure financial terms — it protected the portfolio's long-term trajectory.

Many retirees find that a few hours per week of consulting, teaching, writing, or other flexible work — generating modest income — extends their portfolio's longevity by years. This isn't working in retirement because you have to; it's a deliberate strategy that buys flexibility.

Action Steps

Run the three-scenario retirement calculation for your situation: retiring at your originally planned age, two years later, and four years later. Calculate your estimated portfolio size, withdrawal rate, and monthly income from investments under each scenario. The numbers may surprise you.

Research the phased retirement options at your current employer. Many large employers have formal programs; others will negotiate informally. Even if the answer is no, knowing you asked gives you information.

Estimate your healthcare costs for the period between your planned retirement age and 65. If you retire before 65, this is a real and often underestimated expense. Include it in your total retirement cost calculation.

Think honestly about your job satisfaction. Would extending your career be tolerable, neutral, or actually preferable to full retirement? Are there ways to restructure your work — fewer hours, different role, consulting — that would make staying easier? The financial benefit of working longer is meaningful only if the work itself is sustainable.

Research the "bridge career" concept for your field. Search for roles that use your skills with reduced pressure, more flexibility, and enough income to minimize portfolio drawdowns. Many people find that the transition job they took "for a few years" becomes genuinely rewarding in ways their primary career wasn't.

The Income Growth Strategy: Career Moves That Change the Math

For late starters, the discussion of "working longer" often focuses on the same job, same salary, pushed out by a few years. But there's a more aggressive version of this strategy worth considering: deliberate income growth moves that significantly increase earning capacity in the years you have left.

A substantial income increase in your 50s — through a promotion, a career pivot to a higher-paying field, launching a consulting practice, or developing a high-demand skill — has compounding effects that exceed what simply staying and saving would achieve.

Consider the difference between a 54-year-old earning $75,000 who stays on the same trajectory to retirement at 67, and the same person who invests two years in developing a certification or expertise and moves to a $110,000 role at 56. The additional $35,000 per year in income over 11 years represents $385,000 in pre-tax earnings — and if a significant portion is saved (say, an additional $15,000-$20,000 per year), the portfolio difference at retirement can exceed $300,000.

Income growth strategies worth considering for late starters in their 40s and 50s:

Credential stacking: Many high-demand fields — healthcare administration, cybersecurity, data analysis, financial planning — have certifications that can be obtained in 12-24 months and dramatically increase earning potential. Unlike a four-year degree, these targeted credentials have high ROI timelines compatible with a late-start strategy.

Industry pivot to higher-paying sector: People with core skills in management, operations, HR, finance, or technology can often transfer those skills to higher-paying industries. A project manager in education earning $65,000 with the same skillset might earn $95,000 in healthcare, finance, or technology. The pivot takes effort but can dramatically change the financial trajectory.

Moving to a higher-compensation geography: Remote work has expanded this option significantly. A professional who can work remotely and relocate from a lower-wage market to a higher-wage market — or who can access remote positions in high-paying markets without relocating — may find a meaningful income boost with the same skills.

Asking for what you're worth: Research consistently shows that women and minorities are significantly less likely to negotiate salary than their counterparts. A 50-year-old who hasn't had a genuine compensation conversation with their employer in years may be significantly underpaid relative to market rates. One conversation — supported by salary research from Glassdoor, Levels.fyi, or the Bureau of Labor Statistics occupational outlook — can result in an immediate 10-20% salary increase without a career change.

Social Security as a Working-Longer Incentive

One aspect of working longer that deserves its own emphasis: additional working years don't just grow your savings — they can meaningfully increase your Social Security benefit.

As discussed in Chapter 7, Social Security calculates your benefit based on your highest 35 years of earnings. For a late starter who had low-earning early years, a period out of the workforce, or a career change, additional high-earning years can directly replace lower-earning years in the calculation.

Every year of high earnings after your 35th year of work (or filling in a year when you had zero or very low earnings) can increase your benefit — sometimes by $50-$150 per month, permanently. Over a 20-year retirement, that's $12,000-$36,000 in additional Social Security lifetime income from a single additional year of work.

This creates a reinforcing loop: working longer simultaneously grows your portfolio, delays Social Security claiming (increasing monthly benefit), and potentially increases the base benefit calculation. These three effects together are why even a single additional working year can be worth far more than the salary earned during that year.

Chapter 11: Your Late-Start Retirement Plan — Building the Actual Numbers

Every chapter in this book has been building toward this one. You now understand your starting point, the account types that give you the most advantage, how investing works, the role of Social Security, the costs of healthcare, and the trade-offs around timing. Now it's time to put it all together into an actual plan — your plan, with your numbers, not a generic example built for someone in a completely different situation.

This chapter is the most practical in the book. Work through it with a calculator and your own financial information in hand. By the end, you'll have a complete retirement projection: what you need, what you're on track to have, and what actions will close any gap.

Step 1: Define Your Retirement Target

Before you can know whether you're on track, you need to define "on track" for your specific situation.

Start with the fundamental question: How much annual income will you need in retirement?

A common rule of thumb is 70-80% of your pre-retirement income. This works reasonably well for many people, but it's imprecise — retirement spending patterns vary enormously based on lifestyle, health, housing situation, and what you plan to do.

A better approach is to build from your actual expected expenses.

Retirement expense estimate – monthly:

| Category | Monthly Amount |

Housing (mortgage/rent, taxes, insurance, maintenance)	$
Food and groceries	$
Transportation (car payments, insurance, gas, maintenance)	$
Healthcare (Part B + D + supplement + out-of-pocket)	$
Utilities	$
Travel and leisure	$
Clothing	$
Personal care	$
Entertainment	$
Gifts and family support	$
Other	$
Total Monthly Expenses	$

Multiply by 12 for your annual retirement spending target.

Some costs will go down in retirement: commuting, work clothing, potentially housing if you downsize. Others will go up: healthcare, travel if that's a priority, potentially dining and leisure. Be honest rather than optimistic. People consistently underestimate retirement spending.

Important considerations:

Have you paid off your mortgage? If so, remove the mortgage payment.

Are you planning to downsize? Adjust housing costs accordingly.

Will your children still need financial support?

Do you have expensive hobbies or travel plans you've been deferring?

What does your family history suggest about your health trajectory?

Have you included healthcare costs for the pre-Medicare years if you retire early?

One useful exercise: look at your current monthly spending and imagine your retirement lifestyle. Not the fantasy retirement — the real one you can actually afford and that would genuinely make you happy. For many late starters, a modest and meaningful retirement — home paid off, Social Security income flowing, a small investment portfolio generating supplemental income, time with family and for pursuits they love — is both achievable and genuinely satisfying.

Step 2: Identify Your Guaranteed Income Sources

Guaranteed income sources are dollars you'll receive regardless of what your investment portfolio does. These are your financial floor — the minimum you can count on.

Social Security:

Pull up your ssa.gov/myaccount statement. Record your estimated monthly benefit at three claiming ages:

At 62: $________/month

At Full Retirement Age: $________/month

At 70: $________/month

If married, repeat for your spouse.

Choose a claiming age for this projection (or build multiple scenarios). If you're in good health and can afford to delay, use 67-70 as your base case; use 62 as your conservative case.

Monthly Social Security income (your projection): $_______/month

Pension:

If you have a defined benefit pension from current or former employment, contact the pension plan administrator and request your benefit statement. This will show your monthly benefit at various retirement ages and whether survivor benefits are available.

Many public sector workers — teachers, government employees, military veterans — have pension benefits that dramatically change the retirement picture. A teacher with a $2,800/month pension and $1,800/month Social Security already has $4,600/month of guaranteed income before touching any savings. The portfolio requirement in that situation is far lower than for someone with no pension.

Monthly pension income: $______/month (or $0 if not applicable)

Other guaranteed income:

Rental income (if you own income-producing property), annuity payments, alimony, or other regular fixed income streams.

Total monthly guaranteed income: $______/month

Total annual guaranteed income: $______/year

Step 3: Calculate Your Portfolio Withdrawal Requirement

Subtract your guaranteed income from your total retirement expense target to find the amount your investment portfolio needs to supply.

Annual portfolio withdrawal required = Annual expenses – Annual guaranteed income

Example: If your annual expenses are $60,000 and your annual guaranteed income (Social Security + pension) is $28,000, your portfolio needs to provide $32,000 per year.

Now calculate the portfolio size needed to support that withdrawal sustainably:

Required portfolio = Annual withdrawal ÷ Safe withdrawal rate

The safe withdrawal rate to use depends on your expected retirement duration:

Planning for 30+ years (retiring around 60 or younger): use 3.5%

Planning for 25 years (retiring around 62-65): use 4.0%

Planning for 20 years (retiring around 67): use 4.5-5%

Planning for 15 years (retiring around 70+): use 5.5-6%

Using the example above: $32,000 ÷ 0.04 = $800,000 required portfolio.

Your required portfolio size: $_______

If this number feels impossibly large, don't panic – the next step is projecting what you're on track to have, and the gap between the two tells you exactly what needs to change. The required portfolio is a target, not a verdict.

Step 4: Project Your Portfolio Growth

Now let's see what your portfolio is on track to be.

Gather your current investment data:

Current 401(k) balance: $_______

Current IRA/Roth balance: $_______

Other investment accounts: $_______

Total current invested assets: $_______

Use this formula for projection (or an online compound interest calculator):

Future value = Present value × (1 + r)^n + (Monthly contribution × ((1 + r)^n − 1) ÷ (r/12))

Where r = annual return ÷ 12 (monthly), n = total months until retirement.

For most late-start portfolios, using 6-7% annual return for a diversified stock-heavy portfolio is reasonable for planning purposes (use 5-6% for a more conservative mix).

Worked example:

Current portfolio: $95,000

Monthly contributions: $1,200 (including employer match)

Years to retirement: 18

Assumed return: 7%

Projected portfolio at retirement: approximately $730,000

You can also use Vanguard's retirement income calculator, Fidelity's retirement score tool, or investor.gov's compound interest calculator to run these numbers without manual math.

Your projected portfolio at retirement: $_______

When running projections, run at least two scenarios: one at 7% (your base case) and one at 5% (a more conservative return assumption). The difference tells you how much market performance variability affects your outcome. If even the conservative scenario is close to your target, you're in good shape. If the conservative scenario falls far short, your plan is fragile and worth addressing now.

Step 5: Compare and Close the Gap

Gap = Required portfolio – Projected portfolio

If the gap is negative (your projection exceeds your requirement), congratulations — you're on track, potentially with cushion.

If the gap is positive (you'll fall short), you have a set of levers to pull. Here's a framework for evaluating each:

Increase contributions:

The most direct lever. If you're not maxing your 401(k) catch-up contributions, start there. Every additional $500/month in contributions adds approximately $150,000-$200,000 to a 15-year projection at 7% returns.

Work additional years:

As Chapter 10 detailed, each additional year of work simultaneously adds contributions, allows portfolio growth, shortens the distribution period, and potentially increases Social Security benefits. Calculate the gap under a "retire two years later" scenario.

Reduce planned expenses:

Could you live on $4,000/month rather than $5,000/month in retirement? The difference in required portfolio at a 4% withdrawal rate is $300,000. Even a 10-15% reduction in planned expenses significantly reduces the portfolio target.

Increase Social Security benefit:

Delaying Social Security claiming from 62 to 67 or 70 reduces the portfolio withdrawal requirement substantially. In the example above, if Social Security at 67 is $1,800/month versus $1,300/month at 62, the annual gap covered by guaranteed income increases by $6,000 — reducing required portfolio by $150,000 at 4% withdrawal rate.

Incorporate housing equity:

If you plan to downsize, include a realistic estimate of the net proceeds and add them to your projected portfolio.

Adjust investment allocation:

If you're holding too much in bonds or cash relative to your time horizon, shifting to a more growth-oriented allocation can improve projected returns — but with higher short-term volatility.

Step 6: Build Your Retirement Income Stack

A retirement income plan maps out where your money will come from in each year of retirement. This is often called an "income stack" — you layer your guaranteed income at the bottom and build up from there.

A typical late-start income stack might look like this:

Income Layer 1: Social Security

Amount: $X/year. Starts at age 67 (or your chosen claiming age). Inflation-adjusted annually via COLA.

Income Layer 2: Pension (if applicable)

Amount: $X/year. May or may not have inflation adjustments — confirm with your plan.

Income Layer 3: Portfolio Withdrawals

Amount: Your annual gap, drawn from investment accounts. Strategy: draw from taxable accounts first (let tax-advantaged accounts continue growing), then traditional accounts when RMDs require it, managing Roth accounts for late-life or estate planning.

The withdrawal sequence matters for tax management. Drawing from taxable accounts first (at long-term capital gains rates) while traditional accounts continue growing, then converting traditional to Roth during low-income years, then drawing from Roth when you want to reduce taxable income — this sequencing can add meaningfully to your after-tax retirement income.

Income Layer 4: Part-time or Bridge Income (optional)

Amount: $X/year for the first 3-5 years of retirement. Even modest part-time work reduces portfolio drawdown dramatically in the early years.

Income Layer 5: Reserve Fund

Emergency savings (3-6 months of expenses in cash), HSA balance, and potential home equity as a backstop for unexpected large expenses.

Step 7: The Pre-Retirement Countdown

The final element of your plan is a countdown of specific actions in the years before retirement.

5+ years out:

Maximize all available retirement account contributions, including catch-up

Resolve high-interest debt completely

Build emergency fund to 6 months of expenses

Begin researching healthcare bridge options

Obtain Social Security projections under different claiming scenarios

3-5 years out:

Run detailed retirement projections annually and adjust contributions

Research Medicare plans in your area

Begin estate planning: will, healthcare directive, power of attorney, beneficiary designations on all accounts

Consider meeting with a fee-only financial planner for a comprehensive review

Begin reducing investment risk gradually (shifting allocation slightly more conservative)

1-3 years out:

Confirm Social Security claiming strategy

Select Medicare plan (enroll during Initial Enrollment Period — the 7-month window around your 65th birthday)

Consider Roth conversions if in a low-income year before RMDs begin

Identify any bridge income sources (consulting, part-time work) to deploy in early retirement

Finalize housing decision (stay, downsize, or relocate)

Year of retirement:

Coordinate Social Security claiming with financial plan

Enroll in Medicare during Initial Enrollment Period

Roll any remaining employer 401(k) accounts into IRA if plan options are limited

Establish a systematic withdrawal plan from investment accounts

Set up a spending account separate from investment accounts (draw quarterly or monthly from portfolio into checking)

Sample Plans for Three Late-Start Scenarios

Scenario A: Starting at 50, retiring at 67

Current savings: $40,000

Annual contributions: $18,000 (including employer match)

Projected portfolio at 67: approximately $820,000

Social Security at 67: $1,900/month

Planned expenses: $55,000/year

Gap covered by portfolio: $32,200/year

Required portfolio: $715,000 at 4.5% withdrawal rate

Status: On track with modest cushion

Scenario B: Starting at 55, retiring at 67

Current savings: $15,000

Annual contributions: $25,000 (maxing 401(k) catch-up at 60+)

Projected portfolio at 67: approximately $480,000

Social Security at 67: $2,100/month (higher earner)

Planned expenses: $52,000/year

Guaranteed income: $25,200/year

Gap: $26,800/year

Required portfolio: $596,000 at 4.5%

Status: Gap of approximately $116,000 – close the gap by working until 69 (adds approximately $140,000 to portfolio) or reducing expenses by $400/month

Scenario C: Starting at 58, retiring at 70

Current savings: $5,000

Annual contributions: $2,000/month (focused, high-income career pivot)

Projected portfolio at 70: approximately $375,000

Social Security at 70: $2,700/month (delayed claiming)

Planned expenses: $46,000/year

Guaranteed income: $32,400/year

Gap: $13,600/year

Required portfolio: $210,000 at 6.5% (only 15 years needed)

Status: Comfortably on track – may even have flexibility to retire at 68

Action Steps

Complete Steps 1 through 4 from this chapter with your actual numbers. Use a spreadsheet, a calculator, or a retirement planning tool. The estimate doesn't need to be perfect – it needs to be honest and specific enough to inform decisions.

Calculate your gap (or cushion). If you have a gap, identify which of the five levers (contributions, working longer, lower expenses, Social Security delay, housing equity) is most realistic and impactful for your situation.

Build your income stack. Map out where each dollar of retirement income will come from, in what order, and starting at what age. Seeing it as layers — not just a single account — changes how you think about the security of your plan.

Create a simple one-page retirement countdown document listing the top five financial actions you need to complete in the next 12 months. Prioritize by impact. Put it somewhere you'll see it.

Schedule a meeting with a fee-only financial planner for a one-time comprehensive review of your plan. Bring the numbers from this chapter. A second set of eyes on a plan this important is worth more than the cost of the consultation — especially for identifying tax optimization opportunities and Social Security claiming strategies that aren't obvious from the outside.

Managing Inflation Risk in Your Retirement Plan

Onc of thc most significant risks that retirement projections often underestimate is inflation — the gradual erosion of purchasing power over time.

If you retire at 67 and live to 90, you have 23 years of retirement to plan for. At a 3% annual inflation rate, a basket of goods that costs $1,000 today will cost approximately $1,970 in 23 years. This means your retirement income needs to roughly double over the course of retirement just to maintain the same purchasing power.

Traditional retirement planning accounts for this in two main ways:

COLA-adjusted income sources: Social Security is inflation-indexed. Some pensions include COLA adjustments (though many fixed-benefit pensions do not). These sources protect against inflation without any action on your part.

Portfolio growth: A diversified stock portfolio has historically outpaced inflation over long periods. Stocks represent ownership in businesses that generally pass price increases through to consumers, providing a natural inflation hedge. This is one reason financial advisors counsel against shifting entirely to bonds or cash in retirement — the loss of growth potential can expose you to serious inflation risk over a 25-30 year retirement.

Practical inflation planning: When projecting expenses in Chapter 11, use a 2-3% annual inflation assumption for most expense categories. Healthcare inflation has historically been higher — 5-7% — which is why healthcare costs grow so dramatically in late retirement relative to early retirement. Stress-test your plan: if inflation runs at 4% rather than 2.5% for a decade, does your plan still hold?

Real estate (through your home value or REIT investments) also provides some inflation protection, as property values and rents tend to move with inflation over time.

The Role of Annuities: When They Make Sense

Annuities are financial products that convert a lump sum of money into a guaranteed income stream — either for a fixed period or for life. They're often poorly understood, frequently mis-sold, and sometimes genuinely useful. For late starters, understanding when an annuity does and doesn't make sense is valuable.

The basic appeal: An annuity eliminates longevity risk — the risk of outliving your money. A life annuity pays you every month for as long as you live, regardless of how long that is. This is psychologically powerful and financially meaningful for people who are worried about running out of money in very late life.

The types most relevant to late starters:

Single Premium Immediate Annuity (SPIA): You give an insurance company a lump sum and they immediately begin paying you a monthly income for life (or for a specified period). This is the simplest and most transparent form of annuity. A 67-year-old might convert $200,000 into approximately $1,100-$1,300 per month of lifetime income, depending on current interest rates and whether survivor benefits are included.

Deferred Income Annuity (DIA) / Longevity Annuity: You pay a premium now in exchange for income that begins at a future age — say, 85. These are inexpensive relative to the income they provide, because most purchasers won't live to collect. They're designed specifically to hedge longevity risk in very late life, allowing you to spend down the rest of your portfolio more freely knowing that income is guaranteed if you live past the trigger age.

When annuities make sense:

You have no pension and no other guaranteed income beyond Social Security — adding an annuity creates a floor

You have significant assets and are primarily concerned about outliving them in very late life (a DIA or longevity annuity might be appropriate)

Your health is average or above and you're in a low-interest-rate environment (lower interest rates make the guaranteed return of an annuity relatively more attractive)

When annuities don't make sense:

You have significant pension and Social Security income already — adding more guaranteed income may not be worth the premium

Your health is significantly below average — annuities favor people who live longer than average

You need liquidity — annuity payments typically can't be accelerated, and the principal isn't accessible after purchase

You're being sold a complex indexed or variable annuity with high fees and surrender charges — these products benefit the salesperson far more than the buyer

If you're considering an annuity, get quotes from multiple companies through an independent source like immediateannuities.com, and compare carefully against the alternative of simply holding a conservative portfolio and withdrawing from it.

Pulling It All Together: Your One-Page Plan

After working through the steps in this chapter, synthesize your plan onto a single page. This document should be short enough to actually read and use — not a comprehensive binder, but a living reference.

Your One-Page Retirement Plan should include:

Target retirement date and age

Monthly retirement income target (from Step 1)

Guaranteed income sources (Social Security and pension, from Step 2)

Monthly portfolio withdrawal needed (Step 3)

Required portfolio at retirement (Step 3)

Current portfolio total and projected portfolio at retirement (Step 4)

Gap or cushion (Step 5)

Three priority actions for the next 12 months (from your gap analysis)

Retirement income stack (where each dollar comes from)

Next annual review date

This plan isn't set in stone — it evolves as your income changes, as markets move, as your retirement date approaches. But having it written down and reviewing it annually is what turns a theoretical commitment into an actual trajectory.

The late-start retirement journey is not a sprint. It's a sustained, consistent effort over 10, 15, or 20 years. The people who succeed aren't those who found a secret — they're those who wrote down a plan and kept showing up for it, month after month, year after year.

That's entirely within your reach.

Conclusion: The Life You're Still Building

At some point while reading this book, you probably ran a number and felt a pang — maybe the number was smaller than you hoped, maybe the timeline felt tighter than comfortable, maybe the gap between where you are and where you need to be made you wince.

That's okay. That pang is information, not a verdict.

Here's what that number cannot tell you: it cannot tell you how many Saturday mornings you have left to redirect, how many raises and promotions and income opportunities are still ahead of you, how many spending choices you haven't yet made, or how resourceful you'll turn out to be once you're genuinely committed to a plan. Numbers capture what has happened. They say almost nothing about what can still happen.

What You've Built in This Book

You came in with a vague sense of anxiety and, hopefully, leave with something much more useful: clarity.

You've seen your net worth clearly, perhaps for the first time without flinching away from it. You've understood the real mechanics of compound interest — not the cartoon version designed to shame you, but the honest version that shows what's actually possible with the time and income you have. You've navigated the alphabet soup of retirement accounts and found the ones that work for your situation. You've looked at debt, investing, Social Security, housing, healthcare, and work without letting any single piece of the picture overwhelm you.

Most importantly, you've built a plan with actual numbers. Your numbers, not someone else's.

That plan isn't perfect. No plan survives contact with reality entirely intact. Markets will do unexpected things. Health will surprise you. Career trajectories rarely go exactly as projected. Life will insert itself. But having a plan means having a direction, and a direction you can adjust is infinitely more useful than no direction at all.

The Thing That Actually Determines Your Outcome

After working through a book full of specific tactics and numbers, the honest answer to "what separates successful late starters from unsuccessful ones?" is simple:

Consistency.

Not the size of the initial contribution. Not the perfect account selection. Not the ideal asset allocation or the optimally timed Social Security claim. All of those things matter, but none of them matter as much as showing up, month after month, and making the contributions — even when the market is down and it feels futile, even when something else wants that money, even when you're tired and discouraged.

The people who build meaningful retirement security starting in their 40s and 50s aren't those who made dramatic one-time changes. They're the ones who automated a contribution and never touched it, who reviewed their plan once a year and adjusted it quietly, who resisted the panic of every market downturn because they understood that they were investing for 20 years from now, not this afternoon.

Consistency is boring. That's the point. The boring repetition of the right behavior, compounded over a decade or two, produces remarkable results. Every financial success story you've ever heard that didn't involve a lottery ticket or a windfall was built on boring consistency.

A Word on Shame

If you picked up this book carrying some weight of financial regret — the years you didn't save, the 401(k) you cashed out, the debt you ran up, the decisions that looked very different in retrospect — I want you to put that weight down.

It is very heavy and it is not useful.

Not a single person reading this book made every financial decision they made because they were careless or foolish. They made them in the context of the information they had, the income they earned, the crises they faced, and the life they were living at the time. Hindsight clarity is extraordinarily cheap. It costs nothing to look backward and see the better path. Living forward in real time, with incomplete information and real constraints, is much harder.

You are not behind because you failed. You are behind because that's where life put you. The only response that matters now is what you do from here.

The financial industry has a particular gift for making people feel shame about money — shame about earning too little, saving too little, starting too late, choosing the wrong investments. That shame is often more useful to the industry than it is to you. It drives people toward high-fee products sold by experts who promise to fix what you've broken. It keeps people from asking basic questions because they're afraid of revealing what they don't know.

Setting that shame aside — fully, permanently — is one of the most financially valuable things you can do. Shame paralyzes. Clarity moves.

The Compound Effect of Doing Something

This is the final piece of math I want to share with you, and it's the most important one in the book.

The compound interest that makes retirement accounts grow over time is real. But there's another compound effect that's harder to quantify: the compound effect of making one good decision, which leads to another, which leads to another.

You opened a Roth IRA. Now you're watching the balance grow, and that growth makes the next contribution feel exciting rather than obligatory. You started tracking your spending. Now you notice a subscription you forgot about, you cancel it, and you feel competent and in control for the first time in years. You read your Social Security statement. Now you understand your projected income and you can actually plan, not just worry abstractly.

Good financial habits don't just accumulate money. They accumulate confidence, clarity, and momentum. The first step is disproportionately hard. Every step after that is easier.

This is why starting — even imperfectly, even with a small amount — matters more than having the perfect plan ready. The person who opens a Roth IRA with $1,000 and commits to adding $100 per month is in a fundamentally different relationship with their financial future than the person who means to start when the time is right. Momentum is worth something. It's worth more than the $100.

The Life You're Building

Retirement planning is ultimately not about money. Money is the means — the unit of exchange that gives you the thing you actually want, which is time. Time to do what you choose. Time with the people you love. Time free from the specific anxieties of financial scarcity.

That future looks different for everyone. For some people, it's modest and quiet — a paid-off house, a garden, grandchildren nearby, Social Security covering most of the bills, a small investment account for extras. For others, it's active and adventurous — travel, new pursuits, the projects and passions that a full career never left room for. Neither vision is more worthy than the other. The goal is that your future looks like the life you actually want — not the one financial media tells you to want.

The life you're working toward — whatever it looks like for you — is built one contribution, one decision, one month at a time. It's built by the you that exists today, making choices for the you that will exist at 70 or 75 or 80.

That future self is counting on you. Not to have started at 22. Not to have made every decision perfectly. Just to start now, stay consistent, and refuse to let embarrassment about the past keep you from building the future.

You haven't lost the time. You just haven't started yet.

Start now.

Your First Three Actions After Closing This Book

Open or update your retirement account by this weekend. If you're not enrolled in your employer's 401(k), enroll today — or call HR first thing Monday. If you don't have an IRA, open one at Fidelity, Vanguard, or Schwab before you do anything else this week. The account is the foundation. Everything builds on it.

Set one specific, measurable contribution goal for the next 12 months. Not "save more." A number: $X per month, into Y account, starting on Z date. Write it down. Then automate it.

Schedule one annual review date — same time every year — to update your net worth statement, review your investment allocation, check your progress against the plan you built in Chapter 11, and adjust as needed. One hour, once a year. Put it in your calendar now.

The late start doesn't define the finish. You do.

Appendix: Tools, Calculators, and Resources for Late-Start Financial Planning

This appendix is designed to be used — not just read once and forgotten. Return to it as you work through each phase of your retirement plan. Every resource listed here is free or low-cost, publicly accessible, and specifically useful for the financial situations late starters face.

Section 1: Government and Official Resources

Social Security Administration

ssa.gov

The SSA website is more useful than most people realize. Key features:

my Social Security portal (ssa.gov/myaccount): Create a free account to access your complete earnings history, see projected benefits at ages 62, FRA, and 70, and confirm your Social Security record is accurate. Check this annually — errors in earnings records are more common than expected, and fixing them is easier before you retire.

Retirement Estimator: Allows you to run "what if" scenarios — what if you retire at 65 versus 70? What if your income changes? Available within the my Social Security portal.

Benefits Planner: A detailed resource explaining exactly how benefits are calculated, how spousal benefits work, and how working while receiving benefits affects payments. Find it at ssa.gov/benefits/retirement.

Social Security Statement: A formal document mailed to workers age 60+ who aren't registered online. Shows your projected benefit under several scenarios.

Important: Call your local SSA office (800-772-1213) rather than waiting in line at a field office for most questions. Wait times vary but phone agents can handle most benefit inquiries and corrections.

How to fix Social Security earnings record errors: If you find an error in your earnings history — a missing year, incorrect wage amount, or name discrepancy — request a correction by submitting Form SSA-7008 along with documentation (W-2s, tax returns) to verify the correct figure. Resolving these errors before you retire is significantly easier than after.

studentaid.gov — Federal Student Aid

studentaid.gov

If you're carrying federal student loan debt into your 50s — more common than the financial press acknowledges — this is your definitive resource.

Loan details: Log in to see your exact balances, interest rates, and servicer information for every federal loan you hold.

Income-driven repayment plans: Compare IBR, PAYE, SAVE, and ICR plans. The SAVE plan (Saving on a Valuable Education) replaced REPAYE and offers the most favorable terms for many borrowers, including potentially $0 monthly payments for those with very low incomes relative to debt.

Public Service Loan Forgiveness (PSLF): If you work for a government entity or qualifying nonprofit, you may be eligible for forgiveness after 120 qualifying payments. Worth investigating even if you're only a few years from eligibility.

Loan simulator: studentaid.gov/loan-simulator projects your total payments and timeline under different repayment plans.

Internal Revenue Service — Retirement Plans

irs.gov/retirement-plans

Not the most user-friendly website, but the authoritative source for:

Annual contribution limits for 401(k), IRA, SEP-IRA, SIMPLE IRA, and HSA

Income limits for Roth IRA eligibility and Traditional IRA deductibility

RMD tables and calculation instructions

Rules for rollovers and conversions between account types

The "one-per-year" rollover rule (you can only do one IRA-to-IRA rollover per 12-month period; direct trustee-to-trustee transfers are unlimited and not subject to this rule)

Bookmark the "Retirement Topics — Contribution Limits" page, which is updated every November with the following year's figures.

Key IRS publication for late starters: Publication 590-A (Contributions to Individual Retirement Arrangements) and 590-B (Distributions from IRAs) are the authoritative documents on IRA rules. Dense but comprehensive.

healthcare.gov

healthcare.gov

For anyone retiring before age 65, this is the marketplace for ACA-compliant health insurance plans.

Plan browser: Compare plans by premium, deductible, network, and covered drugs.

Subsidy calculator: Enter your projected retirement income to estimate your premium tax credit. Important: retirement income for ACA purposes includes Social Security, investment withdrawals, and any earned income — but not Roth withdrawals (which have no tax consequence and don't count as income). This distinction matters significantly for planning.

Special Enrollment Periods: Losing employer coverage triggers a 60-day SEP to enroll outside open enrollment.

Open enrollment for ACA plans runs from November 1 through January 15 in most states for coverage starting the following January. Missing this window requires a qualifying life event to enroll.

Medicare.gov

medicare.gov

The official Medicare resource for plan comparison, enrollment, and benefit information.

Medicare Plan Finder: Compare Medigap and Medicare Advantage plans available in your ZIP code, including star ratings (quality), premiums, and covered benefits.

Coverage comparison tool: See what's covered under original Medicare vs. different Medicare Advantage plan types.

Medicare & You handbook: Published annually, the most comprehensive single resource on Medicare benefits and rules.

Enrollment timing is critical: Your Initial Enrollment Period runs from 3 months before to 3 months after your 65th birthday. Missing it can result in permanent premium penalties (10% per year for Part B, 1% per month for Part D).

Section 2: Financial Calculators

investor.gov — U.S. Securities and Exchange Commission

investor.gov/financial-tools-calculators

Free, unbiased calculators from the SEC:

Compound Interest Calculator: Enter starting balance, monthly contribution, interest rate, and time period. Particularly useful for running the scenarios in Chapter 11 with your actual numbers.

Savings Goal Calculator: Work backward from a target — what do you need to contribute to reach $X by retirement?

Mutual Fund Analyzer: Compare the long-term cost of different mutual fund expense ratios. Useful for evaluating your 401(k) fund options.

Vanguard Retirement Income Calculator

investor.vanguard.com/tools-calculators/retirement-income-calculator

One of the best free retirement income projectors available. Enter your current savings, contribution amount, expected retirement age, and draw a projection with Monte Carlo simulation showing probability of success under different market scenarios. More sophisticated than simple compound interest calculators because it models sequence-of-returns risk.

Fidelity Retirement Score

fidelity.com/myplan

Fidelity's free tool projects your retirement readiness as a "score" showing whether you're on track to replace 45%, 67%, or 90%+ of your pre-retirement income. It draws from actual account data if you have Fidelity accounts and connects to external account information you can enter manually. Useful for a quick status check and for identifying which factors have the most impact on your projection.

Open Social Security

opensocialsecurity.com

Developed by financial planner Mike Piper, this free tool calculates the optimal Social Security claiming strategy for individuals and couples by running thousands of scenarios. Enter your benefit amounts, estimated mortality, and preferences — the tool recommends the claiming age that maximizes expected lifetime benefits. Far more sophisticated than the basic break-even calculators on most financial sites.

This tool is particularly useful for married couples trying to coordinate claiming strategies. It factors in spousal and survivor benefit rules that are easy to get wrong with manual calculations.

AARP Retirement Calculator

aarp.org/work/retirement-planning/retirement_calculator.html

A user-friendly retirement calculator that includes Social Security, pension income, and investment projections. Good for people who want a straightforward interface without a lot of technical configuration.

Empower Retirement Planner (formerly Personal Capital)

empower.com

Links to your financial accounts and provides a comprehensive retirement projection, net worth dashboard, and fee analyzer that shows what you're paying in investment fund fees across your entire portfolio. The fee analyzer alone often reveals significant savings opportunities in 401(k)s with high-cost funds.

Section 3: Investment Account Platforms

Vanguard

vanguard.com

Pioneer of the index fund and consistently the lowest-cost option for long-term investors. Offers every major index fund type (total U.S. market, total international, bond market, target date funds). Account minimums vary by fund — many mutual fund minimums are $1,000 to $3,000, but the ETF equivalents (VTI, VXUS, BND) can be purchased for a single share price.

Best for: Long-term buy-and-hold investors who want to set an allocation and leave it alone.

Fidelity

fidelity.com

No account minimums, no transaction fees on most mutual funds, and home of the ZERO expense ratio funds (FZROX, FZILX) — mutual funds with literally zero annual fees. Also has the most user-friendly interface of the major brokerages and excellent research tools.

Best for: Those opening their first IRA, those who want flexibility with no minimum balance requirement, and those who value customer service.

Charles Schwab

schwab.com

Another excellent low-cost brokerage with $0 minimums on most accounts. Schwab's index funds (SWTSX, SCHF, etc.) are competitive with Vanguard and Fidelity. Good robo-advisor option (Schwab Intelligent Portfolios) for those who want automated portfolio management.

Best for: Those who want a full-service banking relationship combined with investing (Schwab has checking accounts with unlimited ATM fee reimbursements, useful for travelers).

Section 4: Debt and Credit Resources

National Foundation for Credit Counseling (NFCC)

nfcc.org – 800-388-2227

Nonprofit network offering free or low-cost credit counseling and debt management plans. NFCC-affiliated counselors are certified and do not work on commission. A debt management plan through an NFCC agency can consolidate multiple credit card payments into one monthly payment at reduced interest rates – typically 6-10% – without damaging your credit the way debt settlement does.

AnnualCreditReport.com

annualcreditreport.com

The federally mandated site for free credit reports. You're entitled to free reports from all three major bureaus (Equifax, Experian, TransUnion) every week. Review your credit reports annually – particularly before taking on new credit or refinancing – to confirm accuracy and identify any errors or fraudulent accounts.

National Registry of Unclaimed Retirement Benefits

unclaimedretirementbenefits.com

Search for unclaimed 401(k) accounts from former employers using your Social Security number. Also try the DOL's Abandoned Plan database at askebsa.dol.gov/AbandonedPlanSearch. Millions of Americans have retirement accounts they've lost track of — it's worth checking.

Section 5: Healthcare Planning Resources

American Association for Long-Term Care Insurance

aaltci.org

Independent organization with a directory of independent LTC insurance brokers and consumer resources including cost comparison data. Their annual cost-of-care survey is one of the most comprehensive sources of long-term care cost data by region.

Medicare Rights Center

medicarerights.org — 800-333-4114

Nonprofit providing free Medicare counseling and information. Particularly useful for understanding your rights if you're denied coverage, appealing Medicare decisions, or navigating complex Medicare situations (coverage gaps, IRMAA appeals, special enrollment circumstances).

State Health Insurance Assistance Programs (SHIP)

shiphelp.org

Free, unbiased Medicare counseling provided by state-funded programs. Volunteers are trained to help you compare plans, understand coverage, and navigate enrollment. Find your state's SHIP contact information through the national directory. This free service is chronically underutilized — SHIP counselors can walk you through Medicare plan selection in your specific geographic area with no sales agenda.

Section 6: Books Worth Reading

"The Little Book of Common Sense Investing" by John C. Bogle

The definitive case for index fund investing, written by the man who invented the modern index fund. Short, clear, and persuasive. Read it before you consider any actively managed fund.

"A Random Walk Down Wall Street" by Burton G. Malkiel

The classic academic argument for passive investing. More detailed than the Bogle book and provides the historical evidence behind the index fund approach.

"The Simple Path to Wealth" by JL Collins

A conversational, accessible book on index fund investing specifically aimed at people who want a simple, actionable approach. Originally written as letters to the author's daughter. Highly readable and directly applicable.

"How to Make Your Money Last" by Jane Bryant Quinn

Specifically about retirement income planning — withdrawals, Social Security, Medicare, and making money last in retirement. More focused on the drawdown phase than the accumulation phase, making it a strong complement to the earlier chapters of this book.

"Your Money or Your Life" by Vicki Robin and Joe Dominguez

A foundational book on the relationship between money and life energy. Particularly valuable for thinking through what "enough" actually looks like and what your retirement needs to provide beyond financial security.

"Die With Zero" by Bill Perkins

A contrarian perspective on retirement planning that argues against excessive frugality in favor of aligning spending with life experiences at the right time. Worth reading as a counterbalance to the pure accumulation focus of most personal finance books.

"Get Good With Money" by Tiffany Aliche (The Budgetnista)

An accessible guide to financial planning that's particularly useful for anyone who feels behind and needs practical, shame-free guidance on building financial stability from scratch.

Section 7: Professional Help Resources

NAPFA — National Association of Personal Financial Advisors

napfa.org

The directory for fee-only financial advisors — advisors who charge flat fees or hourly rates and don't earn commissions from product sales. This eliminates the conflict of interest present when an advisor is paid by the products they recommend.

Useful for: One-time comprehensive financial plans, Social Security optimization analysis, tax planning with Roth conversions, and estate planning integration.

Garrett Planning Network

garrettplanningnetwork.com

A network of fee-only advisors who specialize in hourly consultations — you pay for specific advice without committing to ongoing management fees. Particularly good for late starters who want professional validation of their plan without the cost of full advisory services.

Section 8: Tracking and Budgeting Tools

Empower (empower.com): Free net worth tracking, investment analysis, and retirement planning tools. Connects to your financial accounts automatically and provides a real-time dashboard of your complete financial picture. The retirement planner tool is one of the best free resources for tracking progress over time.

YNAB (You Need a Budget — ynab.com): The best budgeting tool for people who need active help managing cash flow. Particularly valuable for late starters working to increase their savings rate by finding spending to redirect. Subscription-based (approximately $100/year) but users consistently report saving more than the cost within the first month.

Spreadsheets (Google Sheets or Excel): For the one-page financial dashboard described in Chapter 2, a simple spreadsheet remains the most flexible and private option. Your data stays on your device, you control the format, and you can customize it to your specific situation. A template with net worth, income, expenses, and investment balances updated quarterly is often all you need.

Section 9: Key Numbers Reference Chart

| Item | 2025 Amount | Notes |

401(k) standard limit	$23,500	Under 50
401(k) catch-up (50+)	$7,500	Total $31,000
401(k) enhanced catch-up (60-63)	~$11,250	Total ~$34,750
IRA standard limit	$7,000	Under 50
IRA catch-up (50+)	$1,000	Total $8,000
HSA individual limit	$4,300	
HSA family limit	$8,550	
HSA catch-up (55+)	$1,000	
Social Security FRA (born 1960+)	Age 67	
Medicare eligibility	Age 65	
RMD start age (current)	Age 73	Rising to 75 for those born 1960+
IRMAA single threshold	$106,000	2-year lookback
IRMAA married threshold	$212,000	2-year lookback

This appendix will remain relevant even as specific numbers change — contribution limits, Medicare premiums, and Social Security thresholds are adjusted annually. Always confirm current-year figures at the relevant official source before making decisions.

Section 10: Late-Start Financial Planning Checklists

The Getting-Started Checklist (First 30 Days)

Use this list when you're just beginning the process described in this book. Complete each item in sequence.

[ ] Create account at ssa.gov/myaccount and download Social Security statement

[ ] Complete net worth statement (Chapter 2 template)

[ ] Gather all financial account numbers and balances

[ ] Identify all outstanding debts with balances and interest rates

[ ] Calculate monthly income and monthly expenses

[ ] Confirm employer 401(k) enrollment and match details

[ ] If not enrolled in 401(k), complete enrollment form

[ ] Open IRA account at Fidelity, Vanguard, or Schwab if not already established

[ ] Check all retirement account beneficiary designations

[ ] Search for unclaimed retirement accounts at unclaimedretirementbenefits.com

[ ] Enable two-factor authentication on all financial accounts

The Annual Review Checklist

Complete once per year — set a recurring calendar reminder.

[ ] Update net worth statement with current balances

[ ] Review and rebalance investment portfolio to target allocation

[ ] Confirm current 401(k) contribution rate and increase if capacity exists

[ ] Verify IRA contribution made or scheduled for current year

[ ] Review Social Security statement for accuracy

[ ] Review beneficiary designations on all accounts

[ ] Evaluate insurance coverage (life, disability, LTC) for continued adequacy

[ ] Review emergency fund balance (target: 3-6 months of expenses)

[ ] Update retirement projection with current numbers

[ ] Review debt balances and progress against payoff plan

[ ] Confirm Medicare enrollment on schedule (if age 64 or approaching 65)

The Pre-Retirement Checklist (5 Years Before Target Date)

[ ] Run detailed retirement income projection with current numbers

[ ] Determine Social Security claiming strategy

[ ] Research Medicare plan options in your area

[ ] Evaluate long-term care insurance options and cost

[ ] Complete or update estate planning documents (will, directives, POA)

[ ] Review housing plan (stay, downsize, relocate)

[ ] Assess bridge income opportunities (consulting, part-time)

[ ] Calculate healthcare cost budget for pre-Medicare years if retiring before 65

[ ] Consult fee-only financial advisor for comprehensive retirement plan review

[ ] Begin transitioning investment allocation to reduce sequence-of-returns risk

[ ] Establish Roth conversion strategy if applicable

These checklists are designed as starting points. Your specific situation may require additional steps or a different sequence. Use them as a prompt, not a rigid prescription.